JEAN RACINE

By CLAUDE ABRAHAM
University of California, Davis

TWAYNE PUBLISHERS

A DIVISION OF G. K. HALL & CO., BOSTON

Copyright © 1977 by G. K. Hall & Co.
All Rights Reserved

Library of Congress Cataloging in Publication Data

Abraham, Claude Kurt, 1931–
  Jean Racine.

  (Twayne's world authors series ; TWAS 458 : France)
  Bibliography: p. 173–76.
  Includes index.
  1. Racine, Jean Baptiste, 1639–1699. 2. Dramatists, French—17th century—Biography.
PQ1904.A66   842'.4 [B]   77-2377
ISBN 0-8057-6295-7

MANUFACTURED IN THE UNITED STATES OF AMERICA

To the sympathetic duo,
Marcia and Max,
and to two great "sounding-boards,"
Ruby and Ruth.

Contents

About the Author
Preface
Chronology
1. Life 13
2. Racine and Classical Tragedy 26
3. *La Thébaïde—Alexandre* 35
4. *Andromaque* 46
5. *Les Plaideurs* 58
6. *Britannicus* 65
7. *Bérénice* 77
8. *Bajazet* 89
9. *Mithridate* 101
10. *Iphigénie* 112
11. *Phèdre* 122
12. *Esther* 135
13. *Athalie* 144
14. Conclusion 155
Notes and References 159
Selected Bibliography 173
Index 177

About the Author

Born in Germany, raised in France and educated in the U. S., Claude Abraham is presently professor of French at the University of California in Davis. Though his many articles deal with all aspects of French literature, his previous eight books, like *Jean Racine,* focus on the seventeenth century. His *Enfin Malherbe* won the 1970 South Atlantic Modern Language Association Studies Award.

Dr. Abraham has held various offices in a dozen professional organizations and been the recipient of several post-doctoral grants.

Preface

This modest volume is intended for the general reader, the intelligent nonspecialist whose acquaintance with literature has outdistanced his facility with French. Because of this, I have translated all quotations, whether of Racine or of secondary sources, making no attempt to preserve the magnificent poetry of the former or any particular style in the latter.[1]

In the biographical sketch, I have purposefully neglected the usual sequence of daily events for the sake of a more "literary" approach. On the other hand, I have made no attempt to link Racine's plays with his biography, either historically (as did Jasinski) or psychoanalytically (as did Mauron). While I do not deny that the presence of defenseless, pure orphans in so many of Racine's plays (from Astyanax to Joad) may rest upon the fact that Racine was an orphan himself, I have never been able to use that information to obtain a better understanding of either the author or his plays.

Like Raymond Picard, I believe that "nothing is more dangerous than to force [Racine's plays] into a homogeneous mold and to reduce them to a single psychological or dramatic type. No doubt we can discern the lineaments of a certain Racinian technique in his rejections, choices and postulates. On a more ambitious plane, we can doubtless also sense a tonality, a colour and a perfume which we recognize as specifically Racine's. But it is essential to approach each of his tragedies as a world in itself and to avoid one tragedy contaminating the rest."[2] In keeping with that concept, I have tried not to interpret any play in the light of another. On the other hand, like Odette de Mourgues, I do believe in the "autonomy" of Racine, a coherent author who must be viewed as an entity, not as something to be dismembered for vivisection, and like her, I am convinced that for a full appreciation of Racine, his works must be viewed in light of aesthetic norms that were those of his time.[3] In a preface to an edition of *Britannicus*,[4] Philip Butler said, "What Racine reaches for, beyond the confusing world of reality, is truth." In the pages that follow I hope, by focusing much of the light on the distinction to be made between reality and truth, to lead the general reader to a fuller appreciation of Racine. Though stylistic matters have to be largely neglected, as they demand an understanding of French which I cannot assume to be that of every reader, I hope to communicate my enthusiasm for one of the supreme writers of all time, one whose insights into the human heart are as revealing today as they were three centuries ago.

Chronology

The plays are listed according to date of first performance. Dates in parentheses refer to first publication.

1639 Birth of Jean Racine, baptized on December 22. Louis XIV is only one year old at the time, but Corneille, the so-called rival of Racine, is thirty-three and already well established.

1643 His mother having died early in 1641 and his father barely two years later, Jean is adopted by his paternal grandmother.

1649 Studies at Port-Royal until 1653, followed by two years at the Collège de Beauvais. Returns to Port-Royal, 1655–56.

1658 Studies at the Collège d'Harcourt and experiences first literary contacts in Paris.

1660 *Amasie,* his first play, now lost, is accepted and then rejected by the Marais theater. Racine's first poem, a circumstantial ode to the queen, is published.

1661 Works on *Théagène et Chariclée,* a tragedy, perhaps never finished and now lost.

1663 Slips further and further from Port-Royal influence; meets Boileau and Molière; the latter urges him to work on *La Thébaïde.*

1664 *La Thébaïde* (1664).

1665 Great success of *Alexandre* (1666).

1666 Break with Port-Royal: *Lettres à l'auteur des "Imaginaires".* Comments on Aristotle's *Poetics.*

1667 *Andromaque* (1668), again a great success.

1668 *Les Plaideurs* (1669), Racine's only comedy.

1669 *Britannicus* (1670).

1670 The publication of *Britannicus,* along with the first of many polemical prefaces, this one against Corneille, consecrates the "rivalry." Later that year, in November, Racine's *Bérénice* (1671) is performed almost simultaneously with Corneille's *Tite et Bérénice.*

1672 *Bajazet* (1672). Election to the French Academy.

- 1673 *Mithridate* (1673), premiered the day after his official reception at the academy.
- 1674 *Iphigénie* (1675), one of the great successes of the century. This is the year of Boileau's *Art poétique* and of Corneille's last play, *Suréna*. Racine is made Trésorier général de France, a sinecure.
- 1675 Publication of the first collective edition of Racine's theater.
- 1677 *Phèdre* (1677). Named King's Historiographer, another sinecure, but one which will absorb much of his time from now on. Marries Catherine de Romanet.
- 1678 Birth of Racine's first son; five daughters will follow (1680, 1682, 1684, 1686, 1688) before the birth of Louis, seventh and last child, a poetaster and his father's biographer.
- 1685 *Idylle sur la paix*. Corneille having died in 1684, Thomas, his brother, is named to take his place in the academy. His official reception speech is given by Racine who takes the occasion to lavishly praise his defunct rival.
- 1688 Publication of *Hymns from the Roman Breviary*, possibly written as early as the days of Port-Royal.
- 1689 *Esther* (1689).
- 1690 Racine becomes one of the twenty-four "gentlemen of the King's chamber," a valuable sinecure and unprecedented honor for one of such low birth.
- 1691 *Athalie* (1691).
- 1694 *Cantiques spirituels*.
- 1695 Becomes "conseiller-secrétaire" of the king.
- 1697 Complete reconciliation with Port-Royal made manifest by his *Mémoire pour les Religieuses de Port-Royal des Champs*. About that time he composes but does not complete *Abrégé de l'Histoire de Port-Royal*.
- 1699 Death of Jean Racine, April 21. Buried, by his request, at Port-Royal.

CHAPTER 1

Life

I *Formative Years*

JEAN Racine was born in December, 1639, in the somewhat remote town of La Ferté-Milon. His paternal and maternal ancestors were minor administrators. Ambitious and socially conscious, he was always to be irritated by his enemies' constant references to these lowly provincial origins. Rigorous social cleavage dictated that Racine should spend the rest of his days in that dreary and stifling milieu, but Providence was to decide otherwise. Jean was baptized on December 22, 1639; his sister was baptized on January 24, 1641, the mother having died in childbirth. Less than two years later, the father remarried, but on November 4, 1642, at the age of twenty-seven, he suddenly died. His stepmother showing no interest in him, Jean Racine was adopted by his paternal grandmother, who in turn was soon widowed and left in penury. When Racine was less than ten years old, he left La Ferté-Milon, which proved to be a boon in disguise.

When Jean's impoverished grandmother abandoned La Ferté to seek refuge in Port-Royal, she took the child with her. Thus young Racine came to this seat of Jansenist activity in France, the locale of the Petites Ecoles, where he was to get one of the best educations imaginable and make the contacts which would later allow him to make his way in one of the most glittering societies of all time. He studied there from 1649 to 1653; the next two years were spent at the Collège de Beauvais, and in 1655 he returned to Port-Royal. By the time he went to the Collège d'Harcourt, in 1658, teachers such as Nicole, Lancelot, and Le Maître — some of the most erudite men of their time — had given him a rich background, including a thorough knowledge of Greek. The rigor and discipline of Port-

Royal's training were to stand him in good stead later on; at twenty, he felt ready to face a world whose doors had already been opened for him by the more powerful faithful of Port-Royal. By then his first literary attempts were already behind him, though without recognition: he had written some witty letters and some poems, but he had published nothing.

Thanks to the influence of a relative connected with Port-Royal, Racine soon entered the household of the de Luynes family, one of the most powerful of the realm. He quickly adapted to his new tasks and to the glittering society in which he found himself.

By frequenting the worldly poets of Paris, Racine incurred the displeasure of his tutors of Port-Royal, and in 1660 he widened the rift by writing and publishing an ode celebrating the marriage of the king. To understand the distress of his mentors, one must remember that professional writers lived precariously and were not held in high esteem. Society considered it best if one had an "honorable" position on which to rely before trusting in the power of one's pen. The objections of Port-Royal were social as well as spiritual, since they viewed a literary career with alarm. Racine, hurt by their objections, mocked their austerity and spirituality privately and publicly with a biting irony and a lack of gratitude difficult to condone.

This period of worldly activity also saw the completion of Racine's first play, *L'Amasie,* which was initially praised, then harshly criticized and rejected by the actors of the Marais company. Less than a year later he tried again, but friends who read parts of *Théagène et Chariclée* discouraged him from finishing it. Both plays have been lost, but ample testimony is available proving that with them Racine had already elaborated the method of composition he was to maintain all his life: first draw up a very detailed plan of the play before writing a single line of poetry. The failures made one thing clear to Racine: since his position at the Hôtel de Luynes gave him little more than a roof over his head, he had to find a way to earn a living.

In 1661, still in search of material security, Racine went to Uzès, a little town in southern France where he hoped a relative might be able to secure an ecclesiastical sinecure for him. It must be kept in mind that in those days such sinecures seldom meant an accompanying vocation: ecclesiastical posts were most often a matter of finances, not of theology. Racine, avoiding tonsure, became reconciled to the austerity of his new milieu without liking it. He deliberately put up a false front (he used the word "hypocrisy" to describe himself), but in letters such as the ones he wrote to his friend La Fontaine, he showed the persistence of his worldly, literary preoccupations. In this first search for security he showed what everyone soon came to view as an unusually keen eye for politics and reality.

In 1663 this realism won out; Racine gave up trying to find a haven in the clerical ranks and returned to Paris. The timing was perfect: Colbert, Louis XIV's minister, was drawing up a list of writers and artists to be subsidized by the state for the greater glory — and glorification — of the king. Colbert, or more probably his secretary Chapelain, remembered Racine's 1660 ode and put him on the list of royal pensioners. Heartened, the young poet responded with a number of laudatory occasional poems, but it was not until mid-1664 that he received the first payment of his modest pension.

II *The Dramatist's Career*

Meanwhile, Racine had reaped a more important harvest. His reputation growing daily, he attracted the attention of people such as the Duke of Saint-Aignan, one of the wealthiest and most powerful protectors of arts and letters of the century. It was to this patron that he dedicated his third theatrical attempt, the first to come down to us, *La Thébaïde ou les frères ennemis,* commonly known in English as *The Theban Brothers.* Written in 1663, it was performed by Molière's troupe in June of the following year. It has been suggested that Racine resented the date of the premiere, at the heart of the dead season, which possibly was the cause of the lukewarm reception of the play. However, considering that Molière really tried to push *La Thébaïde* by coupling it in performance with popular comedies, it is quite likely that this so-called grudge was invented by biographers trying to give legitimacy to Racine's later behavior.

In November, 1665, Molière premiered Racine's next play, *Alexandre,* which was an instant success. Racine showed his gratitude by also giving his play to the rival troupe of the Hôtel de Bourgogne, where it was performed within days of the Molière premiere. This treacherous act shows that, for Racine, "arriving" took precedence over any other consideration. The Bourgogne troupe was considered the best, and Molière's a distant second,[1] and so the fact that Molière had given young Racine his first chance was not enough to deter the ambitious double-dealer from seeking greater renown. *Alexandre* played on both stages for a while, but when his gate dwindled, Molière soon dropped it from his repertoire. The play was an international success. Almost alone, Saint-Evremond disliked it, or at least failed to join in the general adulation; in this, posterity was to vindicate him, eventually agreeing with him and with Corneille who, in a letter to Saint-Evremond, called the play too *doucereux* ("sweetish"). Corneille, however, overdefended his position when he stated that love is "a passion too full of weaknesses to be the dominant one in a heroic play."[2] Love as the prime mover of tragedy will be Racine's hallmark and the reason for his success. But love is one thing, mawkish gallantry quite another, and it is the latter that eventually killed *Alexandre* in the public eye.[3] Perhaps meant to rival Quinault and Thomas Corneille, both very successful writers of *galanteries, Alexandre* shared the fate of these two writers' works.

The extent of Racine's polemical spirit was revealed about that time by his gratuitous involvement in the "Quarrel of the *Imaginaires*." In a dispute between Desmarets de Saint-Sorlin and Racine's former mentors at Port-Royal, the latter attacked theater as a poisoner of souls. Racine, resenting Port-Royal's previous attempts to keep him away from the stage, took the general attack personally and replied in a series of letters whose viciousness does him no honor. To be sure the letters show already a "Racinian" mastery of the language, but their tone — against people who had educated him and saved him from misery — found few defenders. This, unfortunately, was a trait that Racine would keep all his life: whenever he felt threatened, personally or not, he overstepped all bounds of decency in his rejoinders. Many contemporaries considered his vicious remarks (which even covered some dead ex-benefactors such as Mère Angélique) less an attack on the Jansenist stand concerning theater and morality than a defense of dramatic poets; ambitious of worldly honors, Racine resented the low esteem in which dramatists were held. In short, these contemporaries saw Racine more intent on defending his social standing than his soul. Eventually Racine must have seen that he was not showing an admirable side; though thin-skinned he was shrewd enough to sense that his ruthlessness might alienate precisely the type of people whose esteem he most needed, the *honnêtes gens,* and so, out of political consideration, he refused to be baited into further debate.

The *Imaginaires* quarrel had barely subsided when *Andromaque* premiered at court on November 17, 1667. A day or so later it made an equally triumphal debut at the Hôtel de Bourgogne, with M!le Du Parc, the former leading lady of Molière, playing the titular role. Adding insult to injury, Racine not only switched camps but took with him, as his mistress, the mistress and leading lady of Molière. The play was printed shortly thereafter with a dedication to Henrietta of England, sister-in-law of Louis XIV and unrivaled arbiter of taste at court. Who could dare to criticize a success that had such backing? To the few daring pedants who saw in *Andromaque* a departure from the rules, Racine replied that "the supreme rule is to please."

Now sure of his ability, Racine decided to challenge Molière and, one year after *Andromaque,* brought forth *Les Plaideurs,* a delightful and timely comedy whose sole purpose was to provoke laughter. *Les Plaideurs* had an honorable and lasting success, but Racine must have decided that comedy was neither for him nor for the Bourgogne troupe; at any rate, he never wrote for the comic stage again.

Was it also the lure of challenge that motivated Racine's next endeavor, *Britannicus,* one year later? Called his most "Cornelian" play, it is indeed replete with the Roman grandeur and pomp, the political plotting usually associated with the plays of Corneille. The partisans of that author responded to the challenge and attacked the play in such a way that Racine felt obliged to reply. In his polemical preface he not only gave a point-by-point rebuttal, but he went on to attack the hero of his detractors, Corneille himself. Some have viewed this preface as a personal affront to Corneille which the old master did not deserve; this is only partially true. To be sure, Racine pulled no punches, but why had Corneille, present at the premiere, uttered derogatory exclamations from the very start of the performance? Why had he shown his bad faith by blaming Racine for doing things in the play which he himself did in most of his own? If *Britannicus* was at first unsuccessful, it was surely due to the cabal of the Cornelian clique, and it took their defeat to assure the play the success it deserved.

Exactly one year after *Britannicus,* Racine again entered the arena against Corneille. His *Bérénice* was first performed on November 21, 1670, seven days before Corneille's *Tite et Bérénice.* This, too, can be considered a Cornelian play in that the characters master their passions and follow their duty, but this is a most superficial view; the topic may be Cornelian, but the treatment is not. Many theories have been proposed as to why and how the two rivals presented treatments of the same topic within a week of each other. An improbable one states that Henrietta of England gave the subject to the two authors, thus challenging them to a face-off. Much more plausible is the theory espoused by Raymond Picard, according to which Racine, having found that Corneille was working on the subject, sought a direct confrontation.[4] The battle was decided at the box office where *Bérénice* won a resounding victory. Colbert, in accepting the dedication of the play two months later, showed that the court shared the views of Paris. In the relatively mild preface Racine defended the play against its critics, but made neither direct nor indirect reference to Corneille. Magnanimity came with victory.

This victory was reaffirmed a year later in January, 1672, with the presentation of *Bajazet. Turqueries* were not unknown, and were, in fact, the rage at court, where the success of Molière's *Bourgeois gentilhomme* was in large part due to them, but they were rare in tragedy.[5] The fad, the success of Molière, the simple desire to fit in with the court's tastes — all these undoubtedly contributed much to the decision to write *Bajazet,* a deliberate and total commitment to local color. Going beyond mere matters of decor, Racine created an atmosphere of oppression, cruelty, and omnipresent death which corresponded to the idea the French had of Turkey. His critics reproached him for his Gallic characters, but most people agreed with the defense he voiced in the preface: he strove for historical and psychological verisimilitude, and he found his vindication in the success of the play. As more and more of his former detractors joined the camp of his followers, it became obvious that Racine's victories had not been of limited scope: his entire concept of dramaturgy was accepted by the majority of theatergoers who henceforth considered him the standard-bearer of French tragedy.

One year later, in January, 1673, that fact was again made clear. While *Pulchérie,* Corneille's penultimate play, was having only a minimal success, Racine scored a hit with *Mithridate* and became a member of the French Academy. Now sure of himself, he barely bothered to attack his more stubborn detractors, concentrating in his preface on the exposition of his dramatic canon. Carefully relying on social and political contacts, sure of his talent, he had risked alienating the entire literary world but had won it over. He now found himself in possession of a growing reputation, social standing, and fortune. To his royalties and pension was soon added the revenue from the post of "Trésorier de France," a sinecure, since with the appointment came a dispensation from duties.

Critics are generally agreed that, as Racine's social activities increased and bore fruit, his literary pace slackened. Nevertheless, *Iphigénie en Aulide* was premiered at court in August of 1674. The ladies were in tears, and the king himself praised the author at length. Racine, happy with the court's favor and obviously unconcerned with the "city," let Paris wait nearly five months for a look at the new play. Paris forgave him this slight; one of the great successes of the century, *Iphigénie* played for three months and received a wave of favorable notices. Shortly before that *Suréna*, Corneille's swan song, had barely caused a ripple. There remained only a few adverse critics, mostly partisans of Corneille, and in his preface Racine simply ignored them, feeling that they could no longer harm him. His combative spirit was in no way diminished however, and when two third-rate authors, Le Clerc and Coras, tried to have Molière's troupe perform an *Iphigénie* while his own was still enjoying its initial run, Racine used his powerful influence to have an injunction issued against the rival play. With his typical disregard for diplomacy and social niceties, he then rubbed salt in the wounds by publicly mocking the injured authors, a gratuitous gesture that galvanized his remaining foes.

Their chance for revenge came on January 1, 1677, at the premiere of Racine's next play, *Phèdre et Hippolyte*. Since rival authors frequently wrote in direct competition, rival troupes exploited this fact. Hearing that Racine was working on a new play, one Pradon, whose two previous plays had been performed by the rivals of the Bourgogne players, decided to produce an earlier *Phèdre,* and in three quick months his play was ready. Racine again tried to have an injunction issued, but Pradon had the backing of some powerful people,[6] and Racine had to back down. Having failed on the legal level, he resorted to professional trickery and saw to it that the best actresses of the Guénégaud troupe (formerly

Molière's) refused to perform. Pradon, the underdog, made the most of this and rallied quite a lot of public opinion in the name of freedom of expression. As a result, Pradon's play was able to rival Racine's for a few months. At the height of the rivalry, the "Quarrel of the Sonnets" broke out, and this polemical tangent gave additional life to Pradon's play. A Pradon backer had written a bad sonnet against *Phèdre;* Racine's camp retorted with a virulent attack on the Duke of Nevers. This second sonnet was attributed to Racine, and things could have turned badly for him: true or not, the accusations were leveled at a powerful lord, and Racine was a mere poet. As poem followed poem, Racine (and his ally, Boileau) found himself in increasingly dangerous waters; though innocent of direct involvement, he found himself the target of the anger of nobles who, regardless of their literary inclinations, could not accept the public attacks of a commoner on one of their caste. Through the intervention of the king himself, things were patched up, tempers cooled, and the sonnets were forgotten. In the meanwhile, the public was rendering its verdict at the box office. In the preface of his first edition, Racine wondered if this might not be his best play, "but I will let time and the readers decide its real merits." The verdict was already coming in: the king had it performed repeatedly at court and when, on August 25, 1680, the Guénégaud and Bourgogne troupes united to form the Comédie Française, *Phèdre* was chosen for the inaugural performance.

This preface to *Phèdre* is remarkably sedate; it is even more interesting in another way: reminding the reader that vice, or the very thought of vice, is decried in *Phèdre,* that the dramatic poem's purpose is moral and instructive, he suggests that this "might be a way of reconciling tragedy with a number of persons renowned for their piety and doctrine, who have lately condemned it, and who would undoubtedly judge it more favorably if authors thought as much of instructing their spectators as of entertaining them, and if they followed, in so doing, the true intentions of tragedy." Viewed in the light of other documents on the subject, this can only mean one thing: Racine had buried the hatchet with Port-Royal. This is not as sudden a development as might seem. Nothing is certain about the exact date of the reconciliation, but perhaps as early as 1669 he was well on the way, having renewed relations with some of his former mentors, particularly Arnauld d'Andilly and Le Maître de Sacy. It is very possible that Racine the politician dominated even Racine the proud, and that the poet really tried his best to soothe the ruffled Jansenists.

Phèdre was Racine's last secular play. The question of his "conversion," as some call it, has occupied critics and biographers for three centuries, and the matter is far from settled. Jean Pommier may well be right when he states that Racine, like most courtiers, simply followed trends, and as Louis XIV became more religious — at least in appearance — so did Racine.[7] All his contemporaries are agreed that Racine was a shrewd courtier. What then of the timely reconciliation with Port-Royal? Why must one read into it more than its face value, that is, a simple ceasing of hostilities, rather than a soulful crisis? As Picard has pointed out, nothing that Racine did before or after *Phèdre* is out of character, and the preface quoted above is the type of thing that was common fare. Picard goes further: if Racine had been sincere in his preface when he stated that tragedy writing is a moral work of God, why did he stop?[8] Does the retirement from theater prove a conversion? Was the stimulus spiritual or secular?

III The Courtier

Racine had made his mark, and while Pradon's play had had a momentary success, Racine's had won out. The affair of the sonnets had reinforced a feeling Racine must have had before, that the life of the theater was a chancy thing at best, full of turmoil and dangers; that success did not entirely remove foes who, by birth and station, would always have the power to make him fear. Now entering middle age, Racine married a very sensible woman; the king appointed him court historiographer, an appointment he shared with Boileau; in addition to financial security, this lucrative post gave him a social status that many noblemen envied (few could understand how such a plum had been given to an ex-bourgeois). When the king told Racine to concentrate on his new duties, this man, who had always been socially conscious, was faced with a simple choice: on the one hand, he could disregard the king's wishes and stay with the travails and chicanery of a trade held in relatively low esteem, keeping up a relatively bohemian appearance and continuing to share his mistress La Champsmélé with a handful of others; on the other hand, he could obey the king and concentrate on the more noble and serene task of recording the king's glorious deeds for posterity, opting, in the process, for a life more in keeping with this newly found social status. Any choice but the latter would have been completely out of character for Racine.

His activities during the next few years strengthen this secular theory. Far from neglecting the stage, Racine reviewed and corrected his plays for subsequent editions. In 1685 he welcomed Thomas Corneille to the French Academy with a ringing defense of the stage. Only two years after *Phèdre* he collaborated on an opera, *La Chute de Phaéton,* unfortunately unfinished. On official occasions at court, his plays were most frequently performed as part of the festivities; had his sincere devotion been opposed to their performance, he could easily have discouraged it. On the contrary, he took great interest in some of the Paris performances for which he personally supervised the casting. He continued to write epigrams against his rivals. In 1685 he acted as librettist, collaborating with Lully on an *Idylle sur la paix.* In short, all his activities show not a return to the fold but a move to a better neighborhood. Permanent tenant at Versailles, with entry to the king's apartments, he seems to be guided by ambition, not contrition, a gentleman busy making the king's glory eternal.[9]

Racine still had enemies, for a large number of people saw him as an opportunist, a hypocrite, a thoroughly contemptible person; but as Picard has pointed out, his appointment came at the time of a veritable explosion of Sun-King-cultism; how could even Racine's detractors fail to honor him as one of the two men chosen to transmit the new faith to posterity?[10] There were troubled moments — such as the accusation, in 1679, that Racine had poisoned the actress Du Parc in 1668 — but generally these were glorious times for Racine. Honors, appointments, and sinecures were showered upon him as his family grew. A son was born in 1678; five daughters between 1680 and 1688, at regular two-year intervals; another son, the poetaster and biographer Louis, in 1692. His reputation, like his family, kept growing; though he had stopped writing, he remained king of the stage, more popular than any newcomers or former rivals.

In 1689 Racine returned to the stage with *Esther,* which he called a "tragedy drawn from Holy Scripture" but which he could just as readily have called "opera" or "oratorio." In no way should this return be considered a reversal in form. For some time the court had been moving toward increased devotion and piety, partly under the guidance of the king's morganatic wife, Madame de Maintenon. The latter was patron of Saint-Cyr, a finishing school for impoverished aristocratic girls whose education and amusement included the performance of plays. When they put too much fire and feeling into a performance of *Andromaque,* Mme de Maintenon began to fear for their spiritual well-being and forbade further performances. She then asked Racine to supply something more appropriate. Just as he had supplied a secular opera for a more worldly court, he now accepted — though with misgivings — to write a spiritual one for the edification of the protégées of the pious first lady. Regardless of what he may personally have felt, he could hardly refuse the request of so powerful a person.

Esther, as has often been pointed out, is not a tragedy in what might be called the "Racinian" sense. Its prologue and three acts, with alternating spoken and sung parts, are more lyrical than dramatic, and performances without the beautiful music of Moreau have seldom been successful. Staged with magnificence, *Esther* was an unqualified success. Part of this may be due to the many allusions to contemporary events by means of more or less obvious parallels (Vashti was seen as the fallen Mme de Montespan, Esther as Mme de Maintenon, Aman as Louvois, Assuérus as Louis XIV, and so on). However, most of the success was due to Racine's professionalism. Commissioned in mid-1688 he worked harder than one would have expected for what might have been considered a girls' pastime. As Picard put it, Racine had been selected for the job not only because he was the poet laureate but also because he was an accomplished courtier whose exquisite sense of propriety could be relied upon for this delicate task.[11] Both qualities contributed to the triumph. By November the girls were rehearsing; when the king attended one of the rehearsals, what had been meant as a relatively private and elevating school diversion became a splendid court extravaganza premiered before the king and the court's elite on January 26, 1689. Pleased, the king came back again and again, personally deciding who would have the honor of joining him.[12] Though *Esther* was not performed in Paris for some time[13] (by royal edict it remained the private property of Saint-Cyr and the ladies of Saint-Louis), it rekindled interest in Racine's previous plays.

Delighted with *Esther,* the king asked Racine for another play to be performed the following year. When Racine delayed, *Esther* was triumphantly brought back. This delay in no way slowed down Racine's ascending star and, in 1690, he became "Gentilhomme Ordinaire" of the King's Chamber, one of only twenty-four — an unprecedented honor for one of such lowly origins.

Athalie was not finished until July, 1690. The king attended several rehearsals early in 1691, and on February 22 he brought along James II and his wife, although neither costumes nor stage settings were yet on hand. Shortly thereafter, the much-promised public premiere was canceled. Some saw in this the effect of changing politics. According to them, the story of Athaliah parallels that of the English rebellion, Athalia being William of Orange and Joas representing James III. The international situation having changed, public performances might have embarrassed France. This is probably not the case: had the king been afraid of political repercussions, he would not have allowed the prompt publication of the play which came out in March, 1691.

A much more likely explanation has been advanced by Picard.[14] He suggests that Louis XIV and Mme de Maintenon bowed to the devout faction which saw in the theatrical ventures of Saint-Cyr — however religious the topic — nefarious distractions that disturbed the educational process and perverted the young ladies. Private rehearsals were one thing; public performances, with the ensuing attention and pride, were another. Moreau, who again had composed the music, was dismissed, and even *Esther,* though undramatic, was henceforth performed, as becomes an oratorio, without extravagance of staging.

As the court became more and more devout, so did Racine. Was this true devotion (as he claimed) or hypocrisy (as his enemies did)? The answer lies in his ever-expanding relationship with his former mentors of Port-Royal. His reconciliation had been complete for some time despite the fact that the 1670s, '80s, and '90s were hard time for the Jansenists and Port-Royal, owing to the persecutions initiated by Louis XIV and Mme de Maintenon. Racine, caught between the two factions, was at first prudently lukewarm in his declarations, but he soon took many risks in defending his friends. He seems indeed to have put his courtly Machiavellian science to good use, trying to get the king to relent in his persecution. He became more and more daring in his public show of zeal for Port-Royal, and much of the relative quiet enjoyed by its pensioners during the mid-1690s is due to Racine's diplomatic skill and daring

Life

devotion. At this time he even began to write an *Abrégé de l'histoire de Port-Royal,* a fervent and ringing defense of its frequenters.

It is probable that Racine was, by then, quite sincere. Even Picard, far from sympathetic to the subject of his study, cannot see in works such as the *Cantiques spirituels* mere "literary exercises."[15] Never a theologic pedant, nor a stickler for dogma, Racine now showed a genuine devotion. His zeal for Port-Royal appears less a choice between factions than a defense of deeply and austerely religious people whom he had come to love. This is why he was able to keep — and even solidify — his position at court where he managed to tread that dangerously thin wire until a year or two before his death. At that point there are many manifestations of a growing religious fervor and a corresponding lessening in cares for temporal glory and position. A worsening illness increased his fervor. Late in 1698, sensing that the end was near, he left a court in which his influence and position had barely declined and with which he still kept in touch. On April 21, 1699, he died and, according to his wishes, was buried in Port-Royal.

CHAPTER 2

Racine and Classical Tragedy

I Tragedy

TRAGEDY was born in Greece at a time when the age of myth was yielding to the age of reason — that is to say, the moment when the mystery of the human condition became the province of a more methodical way of thinking which, it was hoped, would lead to a noncontradictory system of identity. Overly simplified this moment of crisis has at times been labeled as one of passage from an age of religion to one of philosophy, from one of faith in the unintelligible to one of confidence in a system that might attain intelligibility.

Later tragedy, particularly in France, but elsewhere as well — think for instance of the minute analyses of reason and unreason in *King Lear* or *The Duchess of Malfi* — arose when the Thomistic edifice crumbled under the blows from the battering ram of Science and Reason. As in classical times, faith in the unknown was replaced by a new faith, one in the autonomy of man and of human capability. Whereas the "mythophile" asked himself questions such as "Whence am I?" or "Where am I going?" the new man confidently declared: "I think, therefore I am." He could then concentrate on discovering WHAT he was. Years ago, Paul Hazard spoke of a crisis of the European mind[1] which he placed at the end of the seventeenth century; that crisis was born a full century earlier, and we owe our great modern tragedies to it.

In other words, it seems to me that tragedy is especially a literature of transition, of crisis, of awakening to consciousness; that is its genius, its splendor, its source of the power it has over us. "Mythologic" thought moves in a cosmos of divine order in which man would like to participate. In that world man's comprehension and definition of himself derive from his comprehension and definition of the myth — which is almost by definition ungraspable. The precarious nature of this stability was amply demonstrated when, in the period immediately preceding the one that interests us, the myth conflicted with the world of reality. Thus, new geographical and astronomical discoveries shook the foundations of a scientific edifice sanctioned by Church dogma. Innocence can never be regained, and post-Renaissance man could no more disregard what he had learned than a member of a jury can disregard a statement that a judge would like to recall. In short, once man had found his myth lacking, he sought answers elsewhere. Like the Greeks of Aristotle's time, the French of Descartes' time found that new locus within themselves.

Tragedy, for Racine and Corneille as for Shakespeare and Webster, is an investigation of the human heart and mind in search of the limits of the human being. Why then is there so much confusion when French and American or English dramaphiles speak of their respective dramatists?

II *French Classical Tragedy*

Too many critics and historians of French classical literature, writing for a public weaned on Shakespeare, begin with an apology. Thus, in his preface to an edition of Corneille's plays, Georges May suggests that *Polyeucte,* called "tragedy" by its author, may not seem like a tragedy unless it is considered in the light of "the less metaphysical concept of tragedy prevalent in mid-seventeenth-century France,"[2] and Francis Fergusson condescends to admit that Corneille and Racine "*thought* their plays were tragedies in the Greek sense."[3]

The problem here is twofold. First, there is confusion of terms, both *tragique* (content) and *tragédie* (form) being translated by the word "tragedy." Secondly, and this is where the English-speaking reader is led astray, critical definitions are often divorced from what Taine calls "race, moment, milieu," that is to say, from the society that created the entity to be defined.

It might be well to glance at the society in which French seventeenth-century tragedy arose,[4] for Shakespeare and Racine belong to two different social orders. Neither one is, of necessity, better or worse, but they are different. All one needs to appreciate either is not to insist on preconceived notions, or more precisely, one should not insist on reading the one with values acquired from the other.

French classical tragedy was not the result of a steady evolution. It owed little to either medieval or Renaissance drama. Humanists had indeed revived the theater of Greece and Rome, but performances of the ancients and of their imitators were largely limited to school exercises. Throughout the sixteenth century literary critics had debated the question of tragedy, but this had led to little new dramatic creation. Translations abounded, as did adaptations, but there is little resemblance between Lazare de Baïf's *Electre* (1537), or even Garnier's *Troade* (1579), and the plays of Corneille and Racine. Jodelle's tragedies are frequently lyrical, always rhetorical and sententious (one may wonder whether they are tragedies or morality plays), but only occasionally dramatic. At the turn of the century Garnier and Montchrestien united genuine poetic talent with a sense of drama, but they were so behind the times, as Jacques Morel has seen, that their edifice crumbled almost immediately.[5]

When historians of French dramatic literature manage to tear their eyes from the writers of dramatic theory and look at the works of the dramatists themselves, they almost invariably come to the conclusion that classical tragedy was not born of the declamatory humanistic tragedy, but rather of the very varied and irregular forms that followed the disintegration of religious and academic theater. Classical tragedy learned from the pastoral about love and from other dramatic genres about peripeteia, action, and spectacle.[6]

This is particularly clear in the works of Alexandre Hardy, perhaps the first dramatic poet to whom the epithet "hack" could be justly applied. In fact, Hardy was proud of writing for pay. He wrote over six hundred plays, mostly for the Hôtel de Bourgogne, THE professional troupe of actors in Paris at the time. Melodramas replete with horror and physical violence, these plays show no concern for the so-called unities, but they do betray, on the other hand, a definite sense of action, drama, and theatricality. Hardy, like Garnier and Montchrestien, was soon to become an anachronism. As France moved away from religious and political internal strife toward law and order, the two leading classes — bourgeoisie and aristocracy — demanded that the arts reflect that trend. Theater, depending for survival on the good will of what was known as "court and city," could not afford to run counter to its tastes. At Shakespeare's Globe the ordinary people may well have been in the majority; not so in France.

More than the theoreticians, the patrons determined what theater would become. As this public moved toward order, decorum, civility, and sophistication, it demanded a literature that would reflect these desires. A dramatist can help to channel taste, but he cannot go upstream and still make a living for very long: theater simply cannot survive in an intellectual vacuum; it needs patrons if it is to be performed. Dramatists then, as ever, saw that they had to strike a responsive chord in both public and powerful patrons. This is where the relatively minor role of the theoreticians becomes obvious: Corneille's *Cid* was a critical disaster, but a popular success. As Guez de Balzac, an acknowledged arbiter of taste, said to one of Corneille's critics, it is one thing to produce a work entirely within the rules; it is quite another to produce one that wins the applause of an entire country. In practical theater terms, this country was made up of the court and the city, an audience of connoisseurs. To succeed with them, literature not only had to communicate, it also had to rely on its audience to do so. This is why the stage and the pulpit — two areas where there is no room for the alienated and the misunderstood — were the two main cogs of classical literature.

What are the basic ingredients of such a literature? In form and content, it is one subjected to rules of order, clarity, simplicity, and equilibrium. Reason and intellect seek understanding by means of a minute psychological analysis of man and his inner life. Equally important is a drive for universality. In this world there is no room for the Romantic idea of the self-centered artist. Individuals and their plights may be portrayed, but only in order to reveal to the viewer some basic truths of human dimension.

This brings us back to the original question: what is tragedy, or, more specifically, what is a French seventeenth-century tragedy? How does it differ from one by Euripides or Shakespeare? Is it "more" or "less" tragic than either? Before coping with these questions it is best to first get rid of a small linguistic problem. The French have two words, *tragédie* and *tragique,* both nouns, both translated by the English word "tragedy." If I may be allowed to coin the word "tragicness" to translate *tragique,* then the problem, divided into its two component parts, becomes a mere matter of definitions.

Tragicness is a dimension of human existence, the result of a conflict between man and God (or the gods, or fate); man's greatness, in the truly Pascalian sense of the word, lies in the rejection of, or submission to, these forces, such rejection or submission being the result of a crisis of heroic transcendence. In such cases, however universal the situation may be, the heroic character is anything but archetypal. In comedy, the miser is the very incarnation of avarice; he is THE miser. Not so in tragedy: Phèdre has sentiments that are recognized as universal, but it is as Phèdre, the individual, that she touches us. Almost by definition, any struggle between an individual and a divinity is settled in advance. In this struggle we witness what Jean Starobinski has called the "exorbitant ambition" of man doomed to defeat.[7] By chance or perseverance, however, man may transcend his earthly limitations; he cannot defeat the powers-that-be, but he may gain insight into the true nature of things. At that moment of recognition he ceases to act. From active human being, he becomes exemplar. As Nietzsche so well put it, "understanding kills action, for in order to act, we require the veil of illusion; such is Hamlet's doctrine, not to be confounded with the cheap wisdom of John-a-dreams, who through too much reflection, as it were a surplus of possibilities, never arrive at action. What, both in the case of Hamlet and of Dionysiac man, overbalances any motive leading to action, is not reflection but understanding, the apprehension of truth and its terror.... The truth once seen, man is aware everywhere of the ghastly absurdity of existence,... nausea invades him."[8] Prometheus may well be tragic, but Sisyphus, especially the "happy" Sisyphus of Camus, is not. As long as these absolute and universal values are not confused with matters of form or of social context, then there is no reason why the French should not appreciate Shakespeare or the English, Racine.[9] To be sure there may be a linguistic barrier, but no geographic or social frontier need keep anyone from understanding the plight of a human being caught between two *présences:* a world that lacks values and is omnipresent, and a divinity, "the only authentic value, but which remains mute."[10] As Tristan L'Hermite's Hérode says, "What is written by Destiny cannot be erased," and Man cannot hope to escape Moira, but who can fail to be moved by the struggle?

What of tragedy? Can it too be described in absolute terms? Like R. C. Knight, I would propose to see "the common seventeenth-century Tragedy in the first place as a Form, which is a species of the genus Drama, subject therefore to such requirements as *vraisemblance* and *bienséance,* which are laws of Drama, and distinguished from Comedy [in that it is] *historique ou légendaire, royale, élevée de style,* and if not *sanglante* [bloody] of necessity . . . at least including that Peril on which Corneille founds his Unity of Action."[11] This working definition places tragedy in the realm of literature and, as such, obliges it to reflect the society from which it comes — race, moment, milieu.

It is here that rules come into play. The best known of these are the rules concerning the three unities — time, place, and action — of which only the last is to be found in Aristotle's *Poetics.* Shakespeare, in that sense, is "Aristotelian"; his characters move readily from city to city, the action takes days, sometimes years, but there is never more than one action. It is imperative not to confuse plot and action. Plot is the arrangement in a particular sequence of the events that make up a story, be it dramatic or other. Action is the "movement or focus of the soul which actualizes its essence moment by moment."[12] In a truly great tragedy such as *Hamlet* or *Phèdre* the two are indistinguishable. To the French of the seventeenth century, however, that was not enough. They evolved a set of rules which may seem restrictive and artificial to some not familiar with the standards of that time, but which had as their sole purpose the safeguarding of two already mentioned concepts: *bienséance* (inadequately translatable as "decorum") and *vraisemblance* ("verisimilitude," with an emphasis on the psychological). These fundamental concepts, and not the pedants' Aristotle, were to make the French insist not only on the unities but on other safeguards of reason and decorum. In *Richard III* wars are fought on stage; *Julius Caesar* asks the audience to imagine the passage of years; Othello crosses the Mediterranean as easily as he crosses the stage. Racine and his contemporaries rejected such dramaturgy, not in the name of Aristotle, but of reason. They wished to create, not a world of illusion, but an illusion of reality; all obstacles to credulity, to full participation, were banished. This does not mean that Shakespeare's audience had a better imagination or that Racine's was too pedestrian to see beyond the material; rather, it suggests that these rules, set down to give the theatrical experience an aesthetic and psychological coherence, were meant to remove everything that was not germane to the exposition of the moment of truth, the one sublime crisis.

When one considers the nature of the public for this theater (aristocrats and bourgeois, many of the latter trying to emulate the former), it is not hard to see why the subject matter for the plays was rather restricted: neither common people, nor their language, had any place in this dramaturgy. Tragedies were to deal with the mighty of the earth involved in momentous decisions. Under these circumstances both *bienséance* and *vraisemblance* dictated that base language and laughter (however episodic) be banished from the stage. To consecrate this harmony and elevation the classical alexandrine verse was soon established as the only acceptable medium of expression.

This did not come about overnight. Mairet's *Sophonisbe* (1634) is generally considered the first "regular" French tragedy, but it is so only if the term is most loosely applied. Tristan L'Hermite's *Mariane* (1636) and Corneille's *Le Cid* shortly thereafter show by their "irregularity" that the trend had just begun. To be sure, *Le Cid* takes place in one locale and within twenty-four hours, but only at the expense of verisimilitude.[13] Racine surely had Corneille's complicated and crowded plots in mind when, in the preface to *Bérénice,* he made this plea for simplicity: "Only what is probable can move in tragedy. And what is probable about a multitude of things taking place in one day that could hardly occur in several weeks? There are those who think that simplicity is a sign of lack of invention. They do not realize that, on the contrary, invention resides precisely in the art of making something of nothing." He had been even more explicit in his first preface to *Britannicus* in which he said that to satisfy the partisans of Corneille "one would only have to deviate from what is natural to plunge into the extraordinary. Instead of a simple plot, with little subject matter, such as one must be which can take place in a single day and which, progressing gradually toward its end, is maintained only by the interests, the sentiments, and the passions of the characters, one would have to fill that very plot with a quantity of events that could only happen in a month and with a large number of theatrical tricks all the more surprising in that they would be less probable...."

This does not mean that Racine failed to appreciate Corneille's contributions to the genre. At the height of the rivalry he was not up to recognizing the older playwright's merits. Later — unfortunately too late, since Corneille had died — he welcomed Pierre Corneille's brother Thomas to the French Academy with these words of praise for the pioneer: "You know in what condition was the French stage when he began his work. Such disorder! such irregularity! No taste, no knowledge of the real beauties of the theater.... Into this chaos, against the bad taste of the century,... inspired by an extraordinary genius,... [Corneille] put reason on stage, but a reason accompanied by all the pomp and all the ornaments of which our language is capable; happily uniting verisimilitude and the marvelous, he left far behind him all the rivals ... who tried in vain, through their discourses and frivolous criticism, to lower a merit that they could not equal." How can one reconcile this statement with those of the polemical prefaces? The truth must lie between the diatribes of polemics and the overly indulgent panegyric, or rather both are true if stripped of the excesses: almost single-handedly, Corneille had created order out of chaos. He had not been the first in the arena, and he was never alone, but only his genius had been able to impose patterns where lesser writers had failed. He was, as Racine suggested, a pioneer, but Racine was not satisfied to merely accept his legacy.

Aristotle had said that the passions depicted on stage should evoke terror and pity; perhaps because of the influence of Senecan tragedies, most of the critics at the beginning of the seventeenth century interpreted that statement to mean horror and pity, but by midcentury pity had won a nearly unanimous victory over fear — or any other feeling such as the admiration championed by Corneille. Going beyond that, Racine, in the preface to *Bérénice,* rejected the need for bloodshed to arouse fear: "It is not necessary that there be blood and death in a tragedy: it is enough that its action be elevated, its actors heroic, the passions aroused, and that everything exude this majestic sadness which is at the source of all pleasure in tragedy." Passion — whether love or its twin, hatred — became the means not only of evoking pity, but of shedding light on the human soul.

In his depiction of crises — in his very selection of them — Racine had succeeded not only in mastering the unities (as Corneille had eventually done) but in making them work for him, in making them become an integral part of his dramatic effect. He saw (as Goethe was to see a century or so later) that a real master reveals himself in his acceptance of limits, in his oneness with them. His topics were chosen so that, rather than restrict him, they would allow him to give preeminence to inner action. Corneille had been proud of his involved plots ingeniously resolved; Racine saw that these could only detract from the vivisection of a soul in crisis. For him, as perhaps for no other dramatist, every element making up a play had one main purpose: "the Intensification of tragic emotion."[14]

CHAPTER 3

La Thébaïde — Alexandre

HAVING failed twice with obscure subjects, Racine turned to the best-known myth of antiquity, that of the house of Oedipus. Well known as a legend and no less so as a literary and dramatic subject, it had been treated countless times before, notably by Aeschylus *(Seven Against Thebes),* Euripides *(The Phoenician Maidens),* Seneca, Statius, up to modern France, with Garnier and Rotrou each writing an *Antigone.*

I La Thébaïde

La Thébaïde ou les frères ennemis (The Thebaid or the Inimical Brothers) was performed at the Palais-Royal by Molière's troupe on June 20, 1664. Though not a great success, it was not the failure that many critics have tried to make it. During 1664 and 1665 the box-office receipts indicate that the audiences were no smaller than those for other plays. Eventually overshadowed by Racine's later production, it failed to maintain itself in the repertory.[1]

In a preface written in 1675 Racine claimed to have patterned his play on that of Euripides. To other predecessors he gave but scant credit: according to him, Seneca "did not know what a tragedy was"; Rotrou had clumsily tied two plots end to end in a single play; others, such as Garnier, were not mentioned at all. In this, Racine's first play to be performed, the action is smoothly exposed, tightly knit, and at ease within the unities; the stichomythic style used to such great advantage by Corneille is here wed to an elegance that was to become Racine's hallmark. But in spite of all that, Racine owed more to his predecessors and contemporaries — even to Corneille, whose political discourses and at times sententious lines are to be readily found throughout *La Thébaïde* — than he cared to admit. None of that is of great importance. What matters, as Jules Brody puts it, is "whether we can view *La Thébaïde* ... as a reinterpretation of an ancient legend, having a different emphasis, a fresh view of human motives, and a reorientation of tragic interest."² As we shall see, we can so view Racine's tragedy.

The original legend has three basic parts: Oedipus unwittingly kills his father and marries his mother; the two sons resulting from this cursed union hate and eventually kill each other; Creon, their uncle, causes the death of their sister Antigone, his own death, and the downfall of Thebes. Racine readily saw that the subject matter was too diffuse, and thus decided to concentrate on one of these three episodes, the middle one. We shall see, however, that he added in a very compact climax the basic elements of the third episode. Such concentration was possible only because the audience was familiar with the legend.

As the play opens the crisis is about to occur. Already past is the entire first part of the legend, and much of the second. According to the wishes of Oedipe, his two sons Etéocle and Polynice were to share the throne, alternating yearly. Etéocle, first on the throne, has refused to step down, and Polynice, with the aid of a foreign army, has laid siege to the city. Créon encourages Etéocle, hoping to take advantage of the quarrel, but Jocaste, mother of the brothers, obtains an armistice during which Polynice enters the city accompanied by Hémon, one of Créon's sons, who is in love with Antigone, sister of the "inimical brothers." When the combat resumes, Ménécée, Créon's other son, misinterprets the pronouncement of an oracle (which had stated that the troubles of Thebes would end only after the last of the blood of the royal house had been shed). He kills himself, hoping that his self-sacrifice will terminate the fratricidal war. Créon publicly espouses peace but privately urges Etéocle not to yield his position. When the two brothers challenge each other to personal combat, Jocaste kills herself in despair. Hémon, trying to separate the brothers to please Antigone, is killed by them just before they kill each other. Now king, Créon courts Antigone who challenges him to deserve her by imitating her; she kills herself and the final curtain falls as Créon dies in the arms of his guards.

At first glance it would seem that Racine, like Rotrou whom he blamed for this very thing, had brought together two stories into a single play, but such is not quite the case. As handled by Racine this is one story, that of the fall of the royal house of Thebes, one single action set in motion by a malediction and nurtured by one single passion, hatred. In spite of political pronouncements — many of which had timely overtones lost to later audiences — in spite of the tender love duets between Hémon and Antigone or the less gentle amorous declarations of Créon, this is a tragedy of physical hatred, of physical violence. One might say that *La Thébaïde* is the story of a prophecy: its pronouncement, the effect of its ambiguity, and its unavoidable fulfillment. Racine frequently referred to the play by its subtitle, *The Inimical Brothers,* but the thrust of the drama is wider. If we were merely to see in the play the story of "inimical brothers," then the last part would indeed be superfluous. However, these brothers cannot fulfill the prophecy: united in hatred they can only destroy each other. It is Créon who, by removing all obstacles — and eventually himself — ultimately becomes both the instrument and the object of the prophecy.

Racine's first performed play is not perfectly unified. Hatred, ambition, discord, the implacability of destiny — each of these has been suggested and logically defended as the central theme of the play. That is in fact one of the major problems: aesthetically, there is no clear focus but a multiplicity of shifting perspectives. It is not a masterpiece, and the above objection, coupled with the inconsistencies of tone, the frequent sententiousness, and repetitive tirades, prevent even the more benevolent critics from comparing it to Racine's later gems; it is nevertheless not a bad play and deserves study if only for the already marvelous ways in which it reveals Racine's burgeoning technique.

One of the hallmarks of Racine is his ability to quickly immerse the reader or viewer in the action. As the play opens, Jocaste gives some urgent orders before reflecting on her situation. Her first thought tells us that the climax is near: "Here are we now, alas, on this accursed day" (19). Both Thierry Maulnier[3] and John Lapp[4] astutely view this as a "formula for the Racinian canon":[5] The entire past is about to dissolve itself into this fateful day; a drama that has festered for years is about to erupt.

The day is indeed accursed, since the drama can come to a close only when the oracle has been fulfilled: "Thebans, to be rid of war, the last of royal blood must, by a fatal decree shed his blood on your land" (393-96). The oracle is of course ambiguous, as all oracles are: just what is meant by "last"? By his sacrifice, Ménécée shows that he interprets it as "last born." Antigone, first to hear the report of the oracle, initially fears that it means "all," but after her cousin's sacrifice she dares to hope that "heaven is satisfied" (617), that this "last miracle" (691) will end the matter. For a moment Jocaste allows herself to be lulled into facile optimism (771-78), forgetting her previous pronouncements concerning implacable fate. Only at the very end of the play are we assured of what we suspected all along, that all the struggles, the sacrifices, the "free" acts, were but ripples before the fatal tidal wave. Antigone and Jocaste were right in the first place: the blood of Laïus was accursed, and all of it had to be shed.

Some years ago Vera Orgel stated that "the originality of Racine lies in his presentation of the apparent liberty with which his characters bring about their inevitable fate."[6] The key — and deceptive — word here is "apparent." With their repeated hopes the protagonists *think* that they act freely whereas they actually perform a predetermined role. Their freedom, their greatness as human beings, lies elsewhere. Between the oracle's pronouncement and its accomplishment, the "action" of the play takes place — the protagonists' conscious or unconscious fulfillments of destiny. As Jules Brody put it, "it is on this process of learning — the reluctant repudiation of a precious illusion — that Racine centers his tragedy."[7]

Throughout the play, the irony inherent in the above-mentioned illusion of freedom is enhanced by verbal irony. Jocaste, despairing of being able to talk her sons out of killing each other exclaims: "They no longer heed the voice of nature" (1032). Both she and Antigone accuse the brothers of being "unnatural." They forget the nature of their blood, that born of an unnatural union, they were born to act accordingly. Jocaste forgets in her exclamation what she herself had said earlier when greeting the sun: "You know that they are issued from incestuous blood and would be astonished if they were virtuous" (33-34).

Jocaste forever wavers between lucidity and self-deception. She views her sons as cursed by her incest (31-34), delighting in crime (114), full of hate (692), hardened and deaf to her pleas (1029-32). In all these instances she understands the reason for their attitude; yet this knowledge never prevents her from hoping that "nature" and consanguinity will prevail for the common good. Therein lies the ultimate irony. Blood — a word omnipresent in this play — has two distinct meanings for the Theban royal household. On the one

La Thébaïde—Alexandre 39

hand, it represents bonds of love, as when Jocaste prays that "Above all else, let blood speak and do its work" (983). On the other hand, it stands for all the evil in the family and the curse attached to it. Thus, when Jocaste provokes a meeting in the hope that blood will assert itself, blood does indeed speak, and the very meeting that was meant to unite them in the peace of love brings them together in the peace of death. Heaven responded to the pleas of Jocaste (974), but there rules an implacable deity that takes delight in the cruelest of ironies. How easily Jocaste forgets her own lessons and warnings: "It [Heaven] feigns to be appeased, then becomes more severe; it interrupts its blows only to multiply them" (688-89). Such delusions, however frequent, cannot last, and, when Jocaste finally realizes the full horror of the situation, she rushes off to kill herself.

Lucidity is not a surplus commodity in this play, as a look at the two brothers will show. On the surface they seem equally blind and impassioned, but that impression cannot withstand close examination. Though critics, in the distant past, disagreed as to which brother was most odious, recent examinations have shown that Racine carefully used one psychological portrait to give relief to the other. P. J. Yarrow has pointed out that Racine went to great lengths to make Polynice more sympathetic. In a perceptive article,[8] he presented four basic types of proof of his opinion: the disinterested characters definitely prefer him; he has sound political views, at least for the time; Antigone, who is likeable, prefers him; and he is generally shown in a better light as one who hates war and loves justice. While agreeing with everything that Professor Yarrow states, I would place the emphasis of the argument on a negative footing: Polynice is less odious than Etéocle, who is a hypocrite imbued with an all-consuming hatred. Nowhere is this more obvious than in the opening scene of act IV. Etéocle, awaiting the arrival of his brother, speaks of *their* hatred. He thus lends his passions to his brother, reaching a paroxysm of fury in one of the fine tirades of the play, asking that his brother detest him so that he could hate his brother. Etéocle here shows his perverted need for his brother; as Judd Hubert has put it, in the features of his enemy each brother sees his own image which, as a result of an incestuous birth, he detests.[9] Roland Barthes says no less: this hatred does not divide the brothers, it draws them together — they need each other.[10] But the hatred of the two brothers is unequal, that of

Etéocle being greater.

Polynice is not always lucid, and "he dies firmly convinced that his cause is legitimate,"[11] but he does not show the blatant hypocrisy of his brother. Etéocle refuses to relinquish the throne: "Thebes has crowned me to avoid its chains and expects through me to see its sorrows end" (107-8). If there is a breach of faith, the fault must be Thebes', and he has no choice but to obey a city that refuses to accept a prince at the head of a foreign army. Etéocle does indeed seem to have popular approval, but Polynice does not believe in popular rule. In a ringing apology of monarchy (that will again be heard in *Alexandre*), he rejects popular caprice as a guide for rulers. Since when is it up to the mob to choose a ruler (475)? For him, Divine justice decrees that he should gain his rightful place (451) regardless of the wishes of an insolent populace (459).

That the political theme is but a subterfuge is readily seen by the rapidity with which Etéocle abandons it as soon as he faces his brother. One of the most frequently used words in this play is "hate," as both noun and verb. Yet Polynice never uses it in connection with his brother whom he considers "odious" (1177), as he does his reign (1165). On the other hand, Etéocle makes constant use of the word. He knows that it has always existed: "It was born with us; and its dark fury entered our heart with life. . . . We were enemies . . . before life . . . in our mother's womb," he tells Créon (915-24). In their blood Heaven instilled the blackest tendencies of hate and love (929-30), and these sentiments are so necessary to Etéocle that he would be sorry were his brother to abandon his claims and thus remove the apparent reason for their enmity (935). This all-consuming passion has only one blind spot: Etéocle believes — he wants to believe — that his brother fully shares it, fully returns it. But this is not so. In all other respects Etéocle is lucid. His sentiments are not of his own making since they are the gifts of what Jocaste ironically calls "the supreme justice of these great gods" (608), but their virulence, lucidly acknowledged and carefully nurtured, is indeed his.

No study of the multifaceted character of Créon can be contemplated without again having recourse to the notions of irony, ambiguity, and lucidity. In some ways Créon is extremely shrewd. He readily sees the source of the brothers' enmity and its implications. Once nature's laws have been broken, excesses are not only possible but inevitable. His cynical appraisal of a situation to be exploited (880-90) resembles that of Shakespeare's Iago. He is the first to understand that the brothers must meet to bring home the harvest of hate (888). Yet there is ambiguity in his posture; when his confidant Attale presses him to explain his reasons for wanting the war to continue, he speaks of many, but that multiplicity shows more shallowness of understanding than complexity of character (III, vi). He bemoans the loss of a son, but readily consoles himself: "By removing a son, Heaven rids me of a rival" (1452). Fatuously dismissing the decimation of the family, he naively believes himself on the verge of total happiness (1422), expecting to escape the all-englobing curse. At times, he feels quite independent of destiny, at others, its puppet. Only too late does he realize — as Athalie will in Racine's last play — that the gods deceived him with a semblance of freedom, an illusion of will; he sees at last that he merely proposed, the gods disposed.

Créon's courtship of Antigone is no less imbued with irony. Antigone is more than a mere prize of war; she is the witness to his success, which Créon so desperately needs to validate all his previous sacrifices. By her suicide Antigone refuses to sanction Créon's career, and how ironic that he, usually so astute, fails to detect the heavy irony of her parting words as she dares him to follow her (1407-20). When the news of her death reaches him, he has a searingly tragic moment of lucidity, understanding the full meaning of Antigone's farewell and the magnitude of the divine malediction. The last spectator of his crimes (1507-12), he dies of fright before the apocalyptic vision.

As I have stated earlier, *La Thébaïde* is not a masterpiece (to the flaws already mentioned one might add those enumerated by Jules Brody),[12] but it is an important play in announcing what are to become Racinian signatures.

II Alexandre

After the relatively tepid reception of *La Thébaïde,* Racine tried to win success by imitating the then fashionable lyric plays of Quinault. *Alexandre,* whose adventurous premiere has been described in the first chapter, was such a success. However, the venerable Comédie Française performed it only three times during the eighteenth century, and only once since then. As we shall see, neither the initial success nor the eventual neglect need surprise anyone.

Alexandre takes place in the camp of Taxile, one of the kings of India poised to defend their realms against the invading Alexandre. Not all these rulers are of equal heart, and Taxile had already shown his true colors by forcing his sister Cleofile into the arms of the conqueror. As the play opens Cleofile makes every attempt to bring her brother entirely into the ranks of Alexandre, but Taxile still wavers, torn between pride and cowardice. Complicating his situation is his love for the proud queen Axiane, who, in her desire for resistance, is ably sustained by King Porus, a rival of Taxile for Axiane's hand and love. Taxile readily understands that Alexandre's insulting offer could never be made to a ruler as proud as Porus, and he sees in that offer confirmation of the low esteem in which he holds himself. Axiane barely masks her contempt in her last attempt to keep Taxile within the alliance. Ephestion, envoy of Alexandre, couches his offer of peace in such arrogant terms that only a craven Taxile can even think of accepting; Porus rejects it as haughtily as it is offered, and Axiane declares her love for him and her contempt for Taxile.

The battle having begun, a happy Taxile tells Axiane of the death of Porus, but he is rejected once again. The victorious Alexandre enters the camp and promises to reward his new allies and forgive his gallant foes. Axiane, thinking Porus dead, pours out her love in spite of Alexandre, who seconds Taxile's courtship. She dares Taxile to be a real king and thus at least to win her esteem if not her love, but Taxile blunders again by threatening to use the power Alexandre has given him. He repents just as his sister brings the news that Porus is alive and counterattacking. Hoping to settle the issue, Taxile confronts Porus and is killed by his rival, who surrenders to numbers without submission of spirit. In an ending that recalls that of Corneille's *Cinna,* Alexandre shows his magnanimity by recognizing Porus and granting him his realms and Axiane. Bedazzled by the beauty of this gesture, Porus is won over and agrees to become an ally of Alexandre.

Despite the several peripeteias, the plot is rather simple, and Racine was quite right when he stated in his preface that the scenes are "well filled" and "coherently linked," and that "the entry of each protagonist is well prepared and its reason obvious." With all its flaws *Alexandre* held the public's attention without the involved plots to which Corneille had accustomed it, and therein lies the im-

La Thébaïde—Alexandre

portance of the play to the modern student of Racine. If *Alexandre* does not yet show us what Racine really wanted to accomplish, it does show what he wanted to avoid.

Many contemporaries of Racine blamed him for a lack of local color; to them, Alexandre did not seem Greek enough, Porus not sufficiently Indian. Yet some contemporaries saw that this was precisely what was needed — that local color must merely be suggested, not bog down the characters and events, so that universality may be achieved. Unfortunately, in *Alexandre,* not only are places and events abstractions robbed of color, but the protagonists as well. The subject of the play is Alexandre's "générosité," made manifest not only by his words and deeds but by those of Porus. The dialectical fireworks that illuminate this may have enchanted seventeenth-century salon goers, but they have little to do with tragicness, and that is why the play is no longer stageworthy.

Nowhere is this more obvious than in the précieux language of the protagonists. Oxymorons, antitheses, and plays on words are the rule rather than the exception. When Cleofile speaks of her "beloved enemy" whose willing prisoner she has become, it is difficult to say whether she is thinking of the shackles of war or of love. The verbal virtuosity — such as the brilliant exchange of ironic sallies between Axiane and Cleofile in act III, scene i — is totally foreign to the tragic mode. No less so is the love duet that ends act III: Alexandre and Cleofile protest their love (as though anyone denied it!), and their exchange is a wholly undramatic dissertation on love that seems to come straight out of the pages of one of the then fashionable précieux novels. By the same token, when Taxile should touch us with his despair his lines are so artificial that they merely call attention to Racine's facility with the idiom of gallantry: "So I burn in vain for an icy heart" (1185) touches the mind, not the heart.

In fact, the language reveals the shallowness of the characters — and of the characterizations. "Objet" was a common précieux term for the beloved, that is, the object of one's love. Taxile, however, uses the word far too literally; he does not realize that an "object" has a will of its own, feelings of its own, and is not just a thing to be possessed. "It" is the object of love, of admiration — perhaps even of hatred — but it is not AN object. He is not alone in this misconception. Alexandre, though a "timid conqueror" (383), feels that women, like crowns, are prizes of war (839–46), and, like

Taxile, he fails to attract because he fails to convince. He is "the perfect gentleman whose beautiful manners and absolute control over every gesture, every word he utters, belong to the drawing-room rather than the military camp."[13] Cleofile appears not as a woman in love, but as a coquette (361-72) who delights in hearing romantic lies, begs Alexandre to tell her that he conquered half of Asia only to reach her (376-80), and demands her freedom in spite of her fear of obtaining it (403-04). Love, to these characters, is a drawing-room game, not a searing passion. In the preface to *La Thébaïde* Racine had deplored that love had had to be relegated to a position of "mediocre effect." In *Alexandre* he put it in the forefront: everyone is a lover; unfortunately no one is capable of eliciting empathy.

Much the same can be said of the heroic side. Both Alexandre and Porus think of themselves as glorious while considering each other vainglorious. They thus reveal themselves as better judges of each other than of themselves. To Alexandre, war is a challenge, a call for personal aggrandizement, and he resents all forms of competition (1025-30). When he asks a foe to surrender without battle, it is not to avoid danger, but to engage that rival-in-glory to demean himself. At first Porus seems to represent the normal pride of rulers. When Taxile tells him that "the people love kings who know how to spare them," he replies "they esteem even more those who know how to reign" (223-24). Pressed on the matter, however, he admits that he truly loves war, that it is for him a way of proving himself. Contemptuous of everyone — though he, too, uses the language of gallant lovers (669-73) — he sees himself as unique in valor and glad of the solitude it implies (539-48). As Antoine Adam has stated, Porus is not defending his country, he is anxious to affront "the conqueror of Asia" because of the glory involved; the defection of Taxile consecrates his glorious solitude and is thus a source of pleasure for the arrogant king.[14]

What is the role of a coward such as Taxile in a world of gallantry and swashbuckling? From the first scene, he seems aware of his failings. He recognizes that if Alexandre seeks his alliance rather than that of Porus, it is because he is marked as the man of a "less resisting virtue" (35). His sister, whom he "sold" to Alexandre, and who now tries to redeem herself by bringing her brother down to her level, accuses him of wanting to be subservient (109). Yet in spite of that partial vision, he insists on being a dreamer. He knows

La Thébaïde—Alexandre

that Axiane wants war,[15] but nevertheless thinks that he can win her by defecting. He even asks his sister to help him deceive himself (93-99). In the words of Axiane he is a wavering soul torn between love and fear, a timid person gullible enough to fall for his sister's ruses (289-92). He not only asks for self-delusion, but is a deliberate — though clumsy and obvious — hypocrite: he is all smiles (731) as he claims that it is his "painful" duty to announce Porus' defeat. Even his death is a denial of heroic and gallant values. When he finally realizes that love cannot come as a gift from Alexandre, it is a tired and beaten Porus whom he challenges (1437-38); does he hope for an easy victory (1473)? This last act seems stupid rather than courageous: how could he have hoped to destroy Axiane's love for Porus by killing her lover? By considering her a prize of war, by his ignoble challenge of her glorious lover, he has branded himself as an outlaw whose crimes are less against India than against a concept of love straight out of the précieux novels of d'Urfé and Gomberville.

Ironically, it is Taxile's sacrifice that leads to the general reconciliation and happiness. Totally devoid of the qualities normally associated with tragic heroes, he nevertheless is the means by which all problems are resolved. In this play, more reminiscent of a Cornelian "heroic comedy" than of a tragedy, it is the most self-deluding character that allows all the other protagonists to live happily ever after in their world of make-believe.

CHAPTER 4

Andromaque

WHEN Corneille took Paris by storm with his *Cid,* he was thirty years old, a veteran of nearly ten plays who had tried almost every genre. At twenty-eight Racine was still searching for a tragic vehicle when both court and city resoundingly announced that he had found it in *Andromaque.* Having presented, in *Alexandre,* the type of men and women that his contemporaries liked to discuss and hoped to emulate, Racine dared to show them the kind of human beings that made up their society, despite its airs and pretensions. The change in background is no less shattering: *Alexandre* had evoked an air of drawing-rooms and gallantry; *Andromaque* evokes the smoking ruins of Troy, a backdrop before which is acted out the destiny of entire nations.

Racine's public had read the *Aeneid,* indeed learned much of it by heart, but for the sake of *bienséances* Racine had to make some basic changes in that account. As a result his *Andromaque* deals, not with the behavior of petty tribal chieftains, but with royalty that more closely reflected the manners and mores of his contemporaries. The play conforms to the myth of Troy, not its history, to the notion the seventeenth-century public had of the characters of that myth and of regal behavior. The entire drama is imbued with a sense of the majesty and grandeur of classical poetry; yet the sentiments are in tune with those of Versailles.

The play takes place in Epirus, at the court of Pyrrhus, son of Achilles, one year after the fall of Troy. Among the prisoners of the young king are Andromaque, the widow of Hector, and her infant son Astyanax. Pyrrhus has fallen in love with the widow and is neglecting Hermione, his betrothed. Alarmed by the situation, the Greek kings send an embassy headed by Oreste, whose mission is to obtain possession of Astyanax, that is, to call Pyrrhus back to reason and duty. However, Oreste is in love with Hermione and hopes to fail in his mission so that he may carry Hermione back to Greece. Everything depends on Andromaque: if she yields to Pyrrhus, he will reject Hermione; if she rejects him, he will "spite" her, return to his fiancée, and surrender the child Astyanax to the Greeks who are afraid of a possible renaissance of Trojan power. As Andromaque wavers, so do all those whose fate depends on her decision. When she finally decides to give up her dream of remaining faithful to the memory of Hector, it is with the secret reservation that once Pyrrhus has pledged to defend Astyanax, she will kill herself. Hermione, neglected once more, asks Oreste to avenge her honor. He agrees to do so on the very altar on which Pyrrhus is pledging his faith to Andromaque, but he comes too late: when the Greek soldiers hear Pyrrhus' treasonable words — by marrying Andromaque he reestablishes Astyanax on the throne of Troy — they rush to execute him. Oreste brings the news to Hermione whose hatred vanishes once Pyrrhus is dead; remembering only her love, she disowns Oreste and "his" action. Bursting into invectives, she rushes off to kill herself on the body of her beloved Pyrrhus. Upon learning of her death, Oreste goes mad and is dragged away by the Greeks, who flee before an angry crowd bent on avenging its king.

Outwardly, the structure of the play is as simple as its plot. There is no question of condensing an action into twenty-four hours or of limiting space. Time is not an issue in a crisis that could happen at any rate of speed dictated by human hearts, and, since the action is centered on a single character, there is no need for movement. It is precisely because of this lack of linearity that the deeper, psychological structure of the play is quite complex. Time and space are not factors in this because both have been effectively annihilated. We are presented with a status quo — a certain equilibrium, however fragile it may be — which an impending decision, or act, will destroy. This destructive gesture, this release from tension — the climactic moment at which all restraint and virtue must yield to passion and desire — casts its shadow as of the first act.

In his frame of mind Pyrrhus could easily "Marry whom he hates and punish whom he loves" (122). This is also true of the other members of the quadrille who seem to wager, not inanimate stakes on inanimate cards, but their fate on the decisions of others. As a result the acts of *Andromaque* are linked not only by a linear plot but also by suspense of a purely psychological nature. Thus, at the end of the first act, Pyrrhus gives an ultimatum to an undecided Andromaque. The second act unfurls at a higher pitch but ends like the first: since Andromaque is still undecided, Pyrrhus "decides" to give her up and return to Hermione. It is not a true decision, however, since it is not based on his own will — he still shows hesitation and afterthoughts. With even greater tension, the third act ends with another ultimatum, as Andromaque goes to Hector's tomb to seek his counsel. In act four, his mind made up (by Andromaque) Pyrrhus dismisses Hermione. This does not, however, release the tension; the suspense is merely transferred from the Andromaque-Pyrrhus couple to that of Hermione and Oreste, and the question is simply restated, but with new principals. Thus restated the drama reaches its climactic moment.

In such a play, the question of the unities need not be raised, for considerations of time, place, and plot become superficial when viewed in their usual context. They are preempted by an inner coherence, a profoundly dramatic unity. For example, the play culminates in a parricide — since that word signified the murder of a sovereign as well as that of a relative — and the very character of Oreste is bathed in the aura. By the same token, the constant allusions to the Trojan war are also part and parcel of the aforementioned unity. As J. D. Hubert — who entitles his chapter on *Andromaque* "The Trojan Revenge" — puts it, every aspect of the bloody climax recalls the bloody fate of Troy; like Hector's father, Pyrrhus dies on an altar, Hermione's death recalls Polyxena's; and Oreste, in his madness, sees rivers of blood that cannot fail to recall "that fateful night."[1]

To achieve this unity the myth has obviously been changed. I have already suggested that its very aura was altered to submit to rules of decorum. Details also had to be changed, some to conform to the tastes of Racine's contemporaries, others to serve the quest for dramatic unity. Thus, in Racine's play, Pyrrhus has not killed Astyanax during the fall of Troy; Andromaque has not been her captor's concubine or given him a child by this union. The most important change, however, may well be that no direct mention is made of Oreste's matricide. The reasons are far from simple. First, of course, there remains the problem of the *bienséances:* if the main duty of the dramatist is to please and to move, how can he do this if his characters shock and repel? Beyond this obvious fact is another one, of at least equal importance. In the version of the myth best known to Racine's public, Orestes is still a child when the war ends; the matricide is yet to come, and the embassy described by Racine impossible. Through his changes, Racine hints at a crime whose memory haunts Oreste, yet never names it. As a result the public, not the author, supplies the notion of murder, a notion which thus contributes to the climate without actually being present. Were it otherwise, the metaphoric unity would be destroyed, as the play would have two actions, two centers of dramatic convolution. In short, Racine had to break with history in order to bring it to life.

It is in this recreation that Racine succeeded splendidly. Sensing that a knowing public would be bored by long accounts of past deeds, yet obliged to superimpose "that cruel night" on this fateful day, he chose to evoke rather than describe. Andromaque is more than a mere hyphen between the living and the dead. The play takes place in Epirus, a full year after the war; it has a *here* and a *now,* but the "ten years of misery" (873) culminating in "that cruel night" (997) are constantly recalled by her, and if the Trojan war is not to be considered as locked into the past, it is because of her. Astyanax, Andromaque's sole reason for living, represents the past, but he also incorporates the future. *Andromaque* depicts a crisis in the life of the former queen; it also depicts the nadir in the history of the royal family and, by extension, of an entire people. For that people, that cruel night had been the gateway to "an eternal night" (997-98), and so it is for her. Astyanax's mounting on the throne of Troy (1512), the avenging of that cruel night in Troy (1592), all are the result of Andromaque's decision, on this fateful day, to sacrifice her blood, her hatred, and her love (1123-24). Her atemporality allows her to melt her past and her present in a single vision of eternity. Georges Poulet is quite right when he states that the tragic moment derives from this very vision: the contingencies of the here and now are abhorrent precisely because they force her to make a decision that violates her faith to a past. She is "possessed by the action of the moment, ... prey to the immediate while contemplating at the same time the causes and the distant end."[2]

Never before had Racine been able to use the language with such mastery to convey the aforementioned mood. Already in *Alexandre* he had made good use of devices pioneered by Corneille, such as repetition, terse ejaculations, antitheses reinforcing the balanced alexandrines,[3] but now he used them for dramatic effect, to evoke a tragic mood. When Hermione cajoles Oreste, deviously trying to manipulate him, the fricative sounds of her speech convey her sinuousness as much as the words themselves: "Le croirai-je, Seigneur, qu'un reste de tendresse/ Vous fasse ici chercher une triste princesse?" (477-78; "May I believe, my lord, that a remnant of love has brought you here to seek a sad princess?"). Likewise, when Oreste questions his cousin and friend Pylade, the alliterative suite of plosives conveys his unsettled nature far more directly than the meaning of the words: "Toi qui connais Pyrrhus, que penses-tu qu'il fasse?/ Dans sa cour, dans son coeur, dis-moi ce qui se passe" (101-2; You who know Pyrrhus, what do you think he will do? What goes on in his court, in his heart?"), and the hissing snakes of the furies' heads are best evoked by the sibilance of Oreste's own exclamation of terror, "Pour qui sont ces serpents qui sifflent sur vos têtes?" (1638). Such alliterations are frequently allied with rhythmic and metrical manipulations to even better convey the idea involved. When, in the opening scene, Pylade tells Oreste of Pyrrhus' failure to bend Andromaque to his will, he says "Et chaque jour encor on lui voit tout tenter/ Pour fléchir sa captive, ou pour l'épouvanter" (111-12; And every day he will try anything to make his captive bend or to frighten her). The second line gives us Pyrrhus' entire attitude in a nutshell, each hemistich perfectly containing one of the halves of his dichotomous method; to reinforce this statement's metrical division is an alliterative play of vowels (é, i, ... i/ ou, ou, ou) whose very sounds convey the feelings involved.[4]

The vocabulary is handled with equal mastery. Critics have at times deplored what they saw as *précieux* language, citing lines such as Pyrrhus' "Brûlé de plus de feux que je n'en allumai" (320; Burned by greater fires than I ever lit), but that is because they failed to see in it anything beyond a platitudinous metaphor of love. It is, in fact, a masterpiece of dramatic distillation. By the very evocation of the Troy whose fires he kindled, Pyrrhus shows the power of his two passions, love and hate; his burning is perhaps due in part to unrequited love, but no less to his conscience and consciousness of the past. This is made manifest when, in the next act, Pyrrhus states that his "victory begins today" (633); to be truly victorious, he needs one more "conquest," one more "prey" — in his mind, war and love become so intermingled that he uses the same vocabulary for the two — and that ultimate prize of war is none other than Andromaque.

The lasting success of *Andromaque* is in large part due to this mastery of the word; the mood, the aura that surrounds the four main characters is sustained as much by the music of the words as by their meaning. But the profound dramatic unity mentioned earlier is due even more to the perfect amalgamation of inner drives and outer forces within each of these young protagonists.

An external impetus (the embassy) has brought Oreste to Epirus. It is his obligation as ambassador to seek a reconciliation between Pyrrhus and Hermione, but his heart hopes that he will fail. "Hope" is the key word here. All too frequently critics have isolated his famous "Je me livre en aveugle au destin qui m'entraîne" (98; I surrender blindly to my destiny which sweeps me off), to make of him a Romantic madman. In the original version, he abandoned himself to his *transport,* to his feelings, but variants notwithstanding, the entire context clearly shows that he speaks of a happy destiny; he comes to seek Hermione, to "win her ... or die" (99-100). He surrenders gladly to his passion. He embraces this hope with a fervor made all the greater by the knowledge that this may be his last chance of happiness. He consistently speaks of unjust gods and adverse fates that have plagued him before, and, while no specifics are given, it is easy for an enlightened audience to bridge the anachronistic gap and link his moments of early despondency to the ultimate recognition of his parricidal fate (1574). Inevitably, his hope is smothered by external forces and by his own latent melancholia. If in the first act he is a capable and even suave ambassador, the repeated shocks take their toll soon enough; in act III we see him falter, and Pylade takes great pains to calm him down. Pylade is wrong to chide him, to tell him that he is "not himself" (710); on the contrary, his real self is finally dominating. Even in that mood he is still basically lucid. Sensing that the gods are both cruel and unjust, he decides to at least "justify their hatred and let the fruit of the crime precede its punishment" (777-78). Let the gods do their worst; let them take pleasure in shaping his misfortune (1613-20), their tortures are nothing compared to those inflicted by Hermione (1643-44). As late as the penultimate scene, Oreste is still lucidly, rationally trying to analyze the situation. He sees his failure as an ambassador as well as his horrendous parricide. Only when he learns of Hermione's death do his senses leave him. When he faints, Pylade orders that he be carried off before he regains his senses. In modern times these last lines of Pylade are frequently omitted to eliminate reference to a regained lucidity. This seems to me a grave error, for a lucid Oreste — interiorizing the legendary furies and accepting his real destiny — and only a lucid one, can be fully tragic.[5]

Like Oreste, Pyrrhus cannot reconcile the dictates of his heart and those of his mind. Because of his new passion, he not only betrays his alliance but his own vows to Hermione. Whatever the reasons for a marriage of state, however young Pyrrhus may be, he is aware of the fact that he swore to be united to Hermione. "I know what vows I break for you," he tells Andromaque (961). To Hermione he admits "that I pledged ... the faith I now give her" (1281-82), and much of act IV, scene v is a confession that, though the union was arranged, he accepted the arrangement and is therefore responsible for keeping it. He thought that he could honor his pledge, but he now finds that love is stronger and he must obey its dictates. It is because Oreste's embassy reminds him of his failure that he takes pleasure in taunting Oreste, first when the latter presents his ambassadorial ultimatum (241-48), then, one act later, when he tells Oreste that he has seen reason and will dutifully surrender Astyanax and marry Hermione: "Hermione is the pledge of an eternal peace; I am marrying her. It would seem that such a sweet spectacle required only the presence of one such as you" (618-20). He is not alone in this attitude; all the suffering characters vent their frustration on those who plead with them. Such is their state of mind that they frequently belabor precisely those they need. Though Andromaque's fate depends on the good will of her captor, she cannot resist the temptation to remind him that his "beau geste" (of saving Astyanax) is not as grand as he would like her to believe since he insists on making her "pay" for it (308). When he tries to frighten her, her sharp rejoinder — "could some Trojan have escaped you?" (268) — quickly blunts his attack since it reminds him of an episode he would rather forget.[6]

Nowhere is the distinction between mind and heart more obvious than in the teeth-gnashing scene that ends the second act in a mood verging on black comedy. The irony of Phoenix's words is coupled with the irony of the situation: Pyrrhus wants to forget Andromaque, but the more he tries, the less he succeeds; Phoenix repeatedly tells him that the best way to forget a woman is to stop talking about her, but to no avail, as Pyrrhus feels the need to wax elo-

Andromaque 53

quent about Andromaque. In his mind he is cured, but not in his heart; as Phoenix so well puts it, "you love, that is enough" (685).

The two men are torn between love and duty, but the women have an entirely different problem. Living in a world ruled by men, they find that even though they would like to heed the call of duty, external forces will not allow them to do so.

In many ways Hermione reminds one of a spoiled child. Her swift changes from elation to despair, from joy to anger, her lack of poise, her naivety are the marks of youth which make her at once maddening and touching. This is only one aspect of Hermione, a virtuoso role that has made — or broken — many an actress, for she is also a proud princess whose very ancestry reminds her of her failure. Granddaughter of Zeus, daughter of the woman whose face launched a thousand ships, how is she to take a rejection that not only is a political betrayal, but one that shows her to be less desirable than an older, widowed captive? More than Andromaque — who still has Astyanax and her memories of Hector — Hermione is truly alone, surrounded by living reminders of her failure. Hurt, she lashes out in turn, and only the intensity of her suffering redeems her in the eyes of the beholder. When Oreste tries to hide his suffering under a diplomatic veneer — "How well you knew, cruel one.... But, Madam..." (825) — she resents his apparent imperviousness, his immunity from pain, and she tries to hurt him by insisting on her impending reunion with Pyrrhus (833). When Andromaque begs for help in her distress, Hermione can only see a chance to hurt the woman who has inflicted pain on her. Andromaque wants only to be allowed to retire with her son, and tries to enlist Hermione's aid to make Pyrrhus assent. Such a plan would clear a path for Hermione's happiness, but she can think only of her advantage over her rival: "If Pyrrhus is to be softened, who can do it better than you?" (884) she asks. Immature, the young princess bent on revenge commits a grave error; her gratuitous act will bring about her own downfall: in despair, Andromaque will respond to Hermione's challenge and bring her plea to Pyrrhus, eventually acceding to his demand.

If Hermione cannot act logically, it is mainly because she does not know how to rule either her emotions or her thoughts, as evidenced particularly in the opening lines of the last act: "Où suis-je? Qu'ai fait? Que dois-je faire encore?/ Quel transport me saisit? Quel chagrin me dévore?" (1393-94; Where am I? What have I done? What must I do? What do I feel? What sorrow devours me?). The inner turmoil, the lack of control or of awareness, beautifully rendered by the rapid questions that chop up the alexandrine, are taken up again two scenes later when Oreste reports the death of Pyrrhus: "Pourquoi l'assassiner? Qu'a-t-il fait? A quel titre?/ Qui te l'a dit?" (1542-43; Why kill him? What did he do? By what right? Who told you?). These breathless outbursts show her blindness, yet two lines later she regains full lucidity: "How could you believe a maddened lover? Could you not read my innermost thoughts?" (1545-46) and thus it is to the very end when Hermione, having blamed Oreste for the loss of her future — not Oreste the obedient instrument of her vengeance, but the ambassador who destroyed a status quo that at least allowed her to dream of possible joys — she rejects him, Greece, her entire past, and consecrates that annihilation of time by immolating herself on the body of her dead lover.

If anything, Andromaque is an even more complex character, for she is not torn between two passions but between two impossible choices to serve a single passion. Marcel Gutwirth sees her as a tender mother.[7] Roland Barthes claims the opposite, basing his contention on the notion that a mother would be ready to do anything to save her child without hesitation.[8] Sentiments analogous to those of Barthes are frequently voiced by Pyrrhus as he tries to seduce his captive, couching his blackmail in a language that is intended to have a maximum effect on her. He constantly reminds Andromaque of her son's precarious position: "It is I who beg you to save him" (957) and a few lines later, "must I embrace your knees for his sake? ... save him, save us" (959-60). Of course, he makes no mention of the fact that it is he who has put a price on his own "generosity," but it is nevertheless hard to picture her at that moment as the tender, loving mother Marcel Gutwirth would have us see.

When she is finally pushed to the long awaited decision, it turns out to be one which only *seems* to save her son: she will wed Pyrrhus, but thanks to what she calls an "innocent stratagem," she will rob him of his prey by committing suicide, once he has promised to adopt and protect Astyanax. One may well question her naivety. When she reveals her plan to her confidante, she asserts that it alone "will save my virtue, and render what is due to Pyrrhus, to my son, to my husband, and to me" (1095-96); it should be noted that this list begins and ends with mention of herself. Moreover, the question of Pyrrhus' reliability must be raised; the man has always been ruled by violent passions and is not known for keeping his word; how will he react to a "stratagem" he may consider far from "innocent"? If Andromaque is serious when she calls him a man of his word, then she is a fool, and nothing in the play suggests that; more probably, she wishes to deceive herself in order to be able to accept the only way out for her as a human being. As William A. Mould has said, "One senses quickly that Andromaque would prefer reunion in death with Hector to survival in Pyrrhus' court; only the need to protect Astyanax keeps her alive. The boy would seem to be an obstacle to her happiness, to her real personal goal."[9] But that too is an oversimplification.

Andromaque's rejection of Pyrrhus is not only the denial of an inopportune courtship. Pyrrhus wants to bring her into a present which he rules, while she wants to maintain her tenuous link with the past. (Ironically, it is those who precipitate her decision who destroy the present and thus allow her to reenter Hector's world.) Her situation is doubly ambiguous. Both Hermione and Pyrrhus are loved (with an unwanted love) and unloved (by the one that matters). Andromaque is also the recipient of a love she cannot return (in spite of her hatred she has a grudging admiration for Pyrrhus), but there the similarity ends: Hector is absent. To be sure, Astyanax is a physical surrogate, but her expression of her love is never colored by any expressions connoting the physical — a connotation that the *bienséances* could not have suffered.

But there is more here than a mere obedience to laws of decorum. Astyanax is, for Andromaque, both symbol and reality. He is son, lover, all that the past implies. Why then is the play not called "Astyanax?" His absence from the stage would not have bothered a public that applauded Corneille's *Mort de Pompée,* a play in which Pompée dominates a stage on which he never appears. It is not so much that we know Astyanax only through his mother's words as the words themselves. To her he is "le seul *bien* qui me reste et d'Hector et de Troie" (262; the only *possession* that I have left). He is not merely passive, but a thing, an object, and Andromaque acts before him as she would before a mirror. This dehumanization is echoed by Hermione and Pyrrhus, who consider Astyanax only insofar as he can be an effective lever in the manipulation of Andromaque (370, 445, 956, etc.). Though Astyanax is both symbol *and* reality, he is flawed in both; he is too young to be a human being of consequence, and he is almost superfluous as a symbol: before going into combat, Hector told his wife "if I die, let Astyanax find me again in you" (1024). These parting words become a charge — for the union of two souls — that neither time nor humans can erode. As Andromaque puts it, how can anyone expect her to betray a husband who believes he survives in her (1077-78)?

When Andromaque finally realizes that Pyrrhus will not yield and that she must be the one to yield (*fléchir* is the often repeated word), the enormity of her sacrifice resides precisely in the realization that for the sake of Astyanax she is immolating far more than what her protagonists may see as love or hatred. Astyanax may be but a mirror, but she cannot live without him. In him, therefore, she must find a receptacle for both the loves that she bears. It is in him that she finds, at last, the strength to sacrifice "blood, hate, and love" (1124). As Mould puts it, "as long as she retains a clear perception of this convergence, Andromaque can resist the facile appeal to maternal sentimentality."[10] Seen in this light her "innocent stratagem" is a surrender to the demands of the world around her. That is the nature of her loss, the surrender of her privileged position. As a result, once her decision has been reached, she seems dead to herself. On the way to the altar, amid universal rejoicing, she is "incapable of love or hate, and seems to obey without joy or protestation" (1439-40).

Melancholy, not grandiloquence, is the prevailing aura of the tragic figure as she gives meaning to her sacrifice. Pyrrhus was unacceptable as a lover trying to supplant Hector. As a king, he had qualities which Andromaque, however begrudgingly, admired. Once dead, Pyrrhus is no longer a threat to Hector, and only the dynastic value is left. This is why Andromaque can readily change from "rebelle" to "fidèle:" "Everything is now under Andromaque's control; she is treated as queen and we as enemies; Andromaque herself, rebellious to Pyrrhus, now renders unto him all the duties of a faithful widow, orders that he be avenged..." (1587-91). As she had — perhaps naively — expected Pyrrhus to be worthy, she now gives meaning to her sacrifice of herself by acting in a worthy manner, but this in no way reduces the magnitude of the sacrifice.

Surrounded by impulsive young fools, Andromaque alone has

survived. Is this the result of her lucidity? Has her rationality had any effect on the actions of others or on her own fate? The answer must be a resounding no. Insofar as morality is concerned, the characters are all "lucid," but the world is meaningless: they all know the difference between right and wrong, but that intellectual process is of no avail against the force of passion. This weakness is recognized by the various characters. "If he does not die today, I can again love him tomorrow," says Hermione of her faithless lover (1201). She is afraid to see into her own heart (428) and is not alone in that fear. Oreste, for instance, "deceived himself" (37) when he thought himself cured of his melancholy due to his unhappy love, and it is only after he lucidly dissects his feelings that he "blindly yields to his destiny" (98). Pylades, speaking of one of the protagonists, depicts them all when he describes "a heart with so little self-control" (120). Hermione regrets that, in spite of her wishes, she cannot love Oreste, the one she "would like to love" (536), and Oreste, who fully understands that "the heart is for Pyrrhus, the wishes for Oreste" (538), cannot regulate his conduct accordingly.

Irony is no less present in the mechanism of events. In spite of what Oreste and Hermione may say, Pyrrhus' death has little to do with their wishes. Oreste may have forgotten the reason for his trip to Epirus; his soldiers have not. They have come, with foreboding, to the altar on which Pyrrhus is about to marry Hector's widow. His words, as reported by Oreste, are of the utmost importance: "I give you my crown and my faith, Andromaque; reign over Epirus and over me. I pledge to your son a father's love; I call upon the gods to witness it, I swear it to his mother. Let his enemies be my enemies as I recognize him as the king of Troy." Oreste continues his report: upon hearing these words the Greeks, enraged, rushed to kill the king, and so large was their crowd that Oreste was unable to strike (1507-16). In other words, Hermione did not dictate Pyrrhus' death, Oreste did not command or execute the sentence. The only passion involved was that of a king who was executed by his allies for treason. The crowning irony is that Pyrrhus, by marrying Andromaque, was doing precisely what Oreste had wanted him to do all along, but with results that are the very opposite of those desired. As Judd Hubert noted, already present in the first two plays, though hidden beneath the frenetic or the romanesque, and now revealed in full in *Andromaque,* is Racine's tragic vision of man: "that of the vanity of all human effort."[11]

CHAPTER 5

Les Plaideurs

EVEN in some of the so-called complete treatments of Racine's plays no mention is made of his only comedy, *Les Plaideurs*. Critics seem embarrassed by this play which does not readily fit into the otherwise rather unified tragic canon of the author. Some simply neglect it, others see it as an "amusement"[1] or a "diversion."[2] The vast majority of the articles written about this comedy deal with it as a mirror of the legal profession of Racine's day.[3] Only recently have a few articles appeared that take a frankly literary look at *Les Plaideurs,* but here again, the reader seeking help in finding the intrinsic merits of the comedy will be disappointed, since these critics see the comedy again as a mirror — a warping one, to be sure — of the tragedies.

This critical neglect is certainly not a reflection of the theatrical success of *Les Plaideurs*. In fact, the success of the play has at times been a genuine embarrassment to certain critics who would have been much happier had the play melted into convenient oblivion. The editors of one French scholastic edition of *Les Plaideurs* categorically state that the play failed in the seventeenth century and was disregarded in the eighteenth. The history of the performances at the Comédie Française alone dispels this illusion. At first the play failed and after two performances was dropped from the repertoire; but it won immediate approval at court, and the city, little by little, joined the growing chorus of *Plaideurs'* admirers. For a while the play managed to maintain what might be termed a modest position, but it grew steadily in popularity, becoming the most popular of Racine's plays throughout the eighteenth and nineteenth centuries.[4] In this century only four of his plays have been performed more frequently, but not to such an extent as to rob *Les Plaideurs* of its title of all-time favorite of Racine's plays.

It may well be that the chasm between the appeal of the play on

Les Plaideurs

stage and the puzzlement it arouses in the critics is due to the latter's preoccupation with the "why" of the play rather than with the "how." To be sure, its very existence is a puzzle, but the very existence of that puzzle should be a warning to rash critics. To many this comedy remains a polemical document. They see in the parodies of Corneille[5] an indirect attack not only on his rival but on Molière, but they neglect to point out that when Racine mocks certain declamatory styles (791 and following), it is more probably his own friends of the Hôtel de Bourgogne that he gently derides. Many people, during Racine's lifetime and ever since, have amused themselves devising "keys" identifying enemies of Racine who are mocked in his comedy, and many of these keys are not devoid of logic or verisimilitude. In his already-noted article Jean Dubu argues convincingly that Racine got much of his information not only from friends with close ties to the world of jurisprudence — Boileau and Furetière among others — and from contemporary sources such as the *Dialogue des héroes de romans* but also from his own troublesome lawsuits which undoubtedly did no little to color his view of the system of justice then available in France; he even cites a case with which Racine was associated that might be the source of one of the funniest episodes of the comedy, namely, the unending and costly suit over a mouthful of hay. The sanest aspect of that article, however, lies in that its author, while shedding much light on some heretofore obscure aspects of Racine's life, never suggests that he wrote his comedy to wreak vengeance upon his literary and personal enemies.

Another source for Racine is Aristophanes' *The Wasps*,[6] but it would be wrong to suggest that *Les Plaideurs* is a simple adaptation of *The Wasps*. Racine gave full credit to Aristophanes in his preface, but in so doing, was he not buying insurance, so to speak, sheltering the more burlesque episodes of his play under the mantle of respectability granted his Hellenic predecessor? The irony evident throughout the play is also present in its preface, as in the passage where Racine states that he would rather imitate Menander — keep in mind that the seventeenth century possessed very little Menander to imitate! — thus making fun of those who judge by rules and reputation (a pedant might never have read Menander, but how could he attack someone "imitating" such a paragon of regularity?). Racine was very sensitive to the moods of his times, and he knew that his contemporaries would have little care for, or understanding of, the Greek legal system. Furthermore, Aristophanesque darts at his foes would be without effect in seventeenth-century Paris or Versailles. He therefore kept a few of the funnier situations, several basic characters, and united these with more modern sources, cementing the whole with his own brand of verbal fantasy.[7]

The plot, like that of *The Wasps,* is rather complex yet full of life: Judge Perrin Dandin[8] has so overworked himself that he has gone completely mad; his mania is to judge everything, and he has even condemned a rooster for not crowing at the right hour. He must now be watched day and night by his son Léandre, his porter Petit Jean, and his clerk L'Intimé. Léandre is in love with Isabelle, daughter of an incurable litigant, Chicanneau. The latter having started a lawsuit against another perpetual litigant, the Countess Pimbesche, L'intimé and Léandre disguise themselves as sergeant and bailiff to introduce themselves into Chicanneau's house. They make the latter sign many papers relating to the suit, including a marriage contract. To get Dandin's permission Léandre keeps his mind occupied by letting him try the dog Citron, accused of having stolen a capon; as the trial ends, Léandre casually asks a theoretical question: if two lovers want to get married and her father has no objection, what is to be done? Dandin gives the obvious answer, "Marry!" whereupon Léandre reveals who the principals are. Dandin, a stickler for the word of the law, will not recall his judgment, nor can Chicanneau rescind his signature. To cap off the general happiness, Dandin pardons Citron in celebration of the wedding.

Les Plaideurs does not have the psychological depth of a Molière play, but there is no indication that Racine even tried to give it that dimension. We will probably never know whether Racine meant his only comedy for "les Italiens," the Italian troupe of actors then in Paris, but there can be no doubt that it is very much in their vein. The main plot, the ruses on behalf of the lovers, the unflagging élan — these are the basic ingredients of the *commedia* that were still popular in France when Beaumarchais wrote his *Barbier de Séville,* and without which there could have been no Cyrano, Molière, or Regnard. Molière added a personal touch of genius. So did Racine: I suggest that it is no worse for being different.

Les Plaideurs is, to some extent, an attack on the seventeenth-century legal profession, an institution sorely in need of the re-

Les Plaideurs

forms that Louis XIV and his ministers were about to begin. Already the year before, in 1667, a "civil ordinance concerning the reformation of justice" had been promulgated, and Racine may well have taken his cue from that, as had Boileau for his Satire VIII. However, timeliness — and the famous "keys" — notwithstanding, so little care has been given to verisimilitude[9] that it is difficult to view the play as a comedy of manners. Allusions to contemporary personalities are so outlandish as to further enhance that notion.[10]

Les Plaideurs is first and foremost a mirthful spree for intellectuals. Racine's detachment is apparent throughout, as both sides of every argument become targets of his iconoclastic parody. Clarac called this play a "divertissement de lettré";[11] he should have said "lettrés," for only those well grounded in language and literature can fully appreciate its literary allusions and verbal gymnastics, many of which are not left unscathed by translation or the passing of time. Thus, during Citron's trial, the victim's head and feet are brought forth to bear witness against the dog; they are immediately impeached, not because they come out of Petit Jean's pocket (to be in one's pocket is to be bought), but because they come from Le Mans, a city known not only for its fine capons but even more for its easily suborned witnesses. Equally difficult to translate are the frequent puns and abuse of legal jargon; yet it is precisely on this abuse that much of the humor relies, not only because such abuse can be intrinsically funny, but because it is by "learning" it and using it with Dandin that those who surround him can finally bring him to do their will, since Dandin will go along with anything "legal": to the already comic device of a judge prisoner in his own house Racine adds the funny notion of that judge submitting, provided the order for his house arrest be couched in a semblance of legal jargon (116).

When bandied about by people of little education, such language becomes even funnier, witness the scene in which Petit Jean acts as a lawyer (675-85), spouting nonsense alternating with the earthy common sense of his native Picardy. It is in the mouth of the simple Petit Jean that the perversion of clichés is at its best. He has come from Picardy to become Dandin's "Swiss," that is, doorkeeper, and will not admit anyone unless bribed. "Swiss" was also the term generally used for mercenaries, and there was a current saying, "no money, no Swiss," which Petit Jean now uses in a completely different context; later on this will lead to further laughter when we see him at work: he gets the money, but still slams the door in the petitioner's face (177-81). Much the same can be said of all the legal maxims he spouts in his opening tirade.

Much of the originality of Racine (especially in those scenes he claims to have merely translated from Aristophanes) lies in this type of verbal fantasy. Robert Garapon views Citron's trial as a five-movement symphony of verbal wit, none of which is in Aristophanes: lines 675-85: a long exordium which starts in tedium and ends in pandemonium, at which time L'Intimé interrupts and Petit Jean falls apart, forgetting his whole speech; 699-702: a brief scherzo whose humor resides in the repetition and the short body of the plea after the overlong exordium; 735-54: another long speech, this time unmitigated gobbledegook, French and Latin, leading directly into the fourth movement, a voluble relation of Citron's crime, leading in turn into a recitation of the "bases" for the entire affair — bases that go back to the beginning of the world. As l'Intimé reaches back to Genesis and describes chaos and void, Dandin, who has succumbed to sleep, falls off his chair, physically punctuating the verbal paroxysm.[12]

Adding no little to this effect are the bold rhythmic innovations in the verse: misplaced caesuras (12, 84, 109, etc.), enjambments and startling *rejets,* isolated words thus thrown into unexpected prominence, as when Chicanneau first spots his future adversary — "But I see coming the Countess/ of Pimbesche" (187-88)[13] — or later that scene, when the key word *plaider* is likewise isolated (235, 257). What at first may seem like sloppy handling of the alexandrine verse, on closer examination is revealed as a careful exploitation of it. In act I, scene vii, for instance, Chicanneau expresses himself quite decently, and the alexandrines flow quite smoothly; suddenly, the lines become chaotic (222); careful reading reveals that the mentality of the speaker has also undergone a change, and the brutalizing effect of this new rhythm and of the inner rhymes and assonances are but a reflection of Chicanneau's rising excitement. As the scene lapses into rapid stichomythia, the dialogue is metamorphosed into parallel monologues, the lack of rhythmic harmony echoing the lost understanding between the protagonists.

Much the same can be said of the value of words. Note what happens to the meaning of *monsieur* in the following scene, as Chicanneau tries to get past Petit Jean to see the judge: "May I see mon-

Les Plaideurs

sieur?—No.—Could I say a word to monsieur his secretary?— No. — And monsieur his doorkeeper? — That's me. — Please have a drink to my health, monsieur'' (177-80). The word which at the outset is used to identify the master of the house ends up being applied to Petit Jean. It seems at first to have lost all meaning, but has it? Who is the real master? Does this verbal metamorphosis weaken our belief in the meaning of words, or does it rather suggest the presence of a new reality behind the more obvious one? As Chicanneau remarks, the world has changed indeed, and nothing is as it once was or was thought to be (182 sq).

If there is an answer to this riddle, it is to be found in the characters of the play, however lacking in depth they might be. As far as the plot is concerned, the love intrigue is carefully interwoven with that of the litigants and with the running satirical commentary, but the lovers (and their servants) and the litigants do not belong to the same world. Isabelle and Léandre have a firm grasp on reality, and, in order to survive, they must manipulate their monomaniacal elders. The servants, strange mixtures of naivety and cleverness, though imbued with a certain verve, have little life of their own and are therefore tools to be manipulated by the young lovers. We thus have a series of plays within the play during which the "actors" are frequently unaware of their puppetlike behavior, and it is to this blissful ignorance that much of the laughter is due, as the reader and viewer benevolently approve from an omniscient position. Isabelle and Léandre are typical of the lovers of the *commedia,* but, coming after Molière's Agnès, Isabelle strikes us as a rather vapid ingénue. Like her *commedia* and Molieresque counterparts, she is not as innocent as she pretends (341-42) and is quick to face danger (365), but her triumph in these deceptions is due to the stupidity of the monomaniacs rather than to the sharpness of her wit. Léandre capably manages the intrigue but never gains substance as a character in the play.

By comparison the three monomaniacs, though locked into their illusory world, are endowed with a certain relief. As mechanical as any of Molière's monomaniacs (Harpagon has just been created), these characters are not totally devoid of rationality — Dandin, for instance, sees law as a great equalizer: gentlemen have to wait at his door like beggars — but whatever that rationality may be, it must yield before the demands of the mania. Dandin is so in love with law that, though he knows his son is wrong to command him, he will submit provided the command is couched in the proper legal language (116–17). Devious, with a totally perverted sense of right and wrong,[14] Chicanneau has amassed wealth; yet he has changed residence just to live near a judge, and for two bales of hay he has started a lawsuit that will cost him a fortune (206–34); whenever he gets fooled (II, iii, iv, vi), it is because his mania supplants his reason or stifles his perception. The countess is suing her husband, her father, and her children; they have given her an ample pension but forbidden her to sue, "But living without suing, is that a life?" (250). When they meet, they are kindred souls; differences in station disappear: "How long have you been litigating? — Thirty years. — That's not too long. — Alas!" (254). Ironically, it is this common trait which prevents any harmony from existing for any length of time, and soon they move from agreement to disagreement, and to the inevitable: they will sue one another. As in his tragedies, Racine has put us in the presence of characters who cannot communicate.

Does this imply that the comedy has tragic overtones? Far from it. As Nathan Gross has said, "The play takes its place in the Racinian canon as an exploration from a comic angle of serious problems Racine had treated and was to deal with again. Racine seems to have indulged in facetiousness at his own expense by parodying elements of his own tragic dramas. This is a Racine who is not to appear again, a poet smiling at his craft, amusing and diverting himself by fashioning a comedy with materials capable of evoking pity and fear." No less important is the statement he had made earlier: "The comic characters have lost their humanity, obsessed with pleading and judging; Néron [of the next play] viciously tramples it underfoot."[15] Unlike the world of Andromaque or of Néron this is one in which human design and planning can win; all that is necessary for everyone to be happy — and it must be noted that Léandre wants even his father to be happy — is that someone be capable of reconciling the real and the illusory worlds. That is the lesson of every play of Molière involving a harmless monomaniac; it is no less the lesson of *Les Plaideurs*.

CHAPTER 6

Britannicus

AFTER the success of *Andromaque* the partisans of Corneille granted that Racine had the talent to write a play about passions, but they still denied that he knew how to dramatize political and historical matter. Racine obviously wrote *Britannicus* in answer to that challenge to prove that he could rival Corneille on the latter's ground. The poor reception of the play embittered Racine who published it with one of his most vehemently polemical prefaces in which he likened himself to Terence obliged to defend himself against an ill-intentioned old poet. When Boileau censured the tone of that preface, Racine removed its most virulent parts in subsequent editions.

The plot of *Britannicus* is extremely simple, drawn from the *Annals* of Tacitus. Dowager Empress Agrippine has put Néron on the throne in place of the rightful ruler, his half-brother Britannicus. As the play opens Néron has arranged for the abduction of Junie, great-granddaughter of Augustus and beloved of Britannicus. Burrhus, one of Néron's tutors, sees reasons of state behind the move: if Britannicus and Junie were to marry, their legitimate claims to the throne might be difficult to refute. Moreover, Néron has fallen in love with his captive, and he tries in vain to take the place of Britannicus in her heart. Failing, he has Britannicus arrested and the ever-meddling Agrippine put under house arrest. His own personality and his evil adviser Narcisse take over and, at the feast of reconciliation, he poisons Britannicus as Junie flees to the Vestal Virgins.

Not all of the above comes from Tacitus: there is little resemblance between Junie and the historical Junia Calvina; the real Narcissus had been killed at the start of Nero's reign; Burrhus had been a rough and tough soldier without scruples or squeamishness, a far cry from the character Racine needed to balance his Narcisse. Racine's greatest claim to originality, however, lies in the creation of the mood, the description of the vipers' nest, the vivid representation of the tangle of passions and ambitions. The subject matter may be Cornelian, but the treatment is not. Corneille evoked the grandeur of Rome, Racine its decadence; Corneille painted enormous frescoes that demanded admiration, Racine gave such depth to a more economical painting that it makes us recoil in horror. Certain themes recall the dramaturgy of Corneille, who, long before *Suréna*, had shown the pressures put by Machiavellian compromisers on the pure. Whereas Corneille had the latter reject such compromises — "I will take care of my glory, do as you will with my life," says Suréna to his frustrated king — and either die (Suréna) or suffer in endless isolation (Horace), here it is otherwise. The oppressive mood overhanging *Britannicus* is in large part due to the obvious fact that not only do the evil protagonists of this play masquerade as virtuous, but that they force the good to forsake their stand. As we witness this ineluctable erosion of virtue, the "decornelianization" of the theme becomes evident: a Rodogune may try to pit son against son, but they refuse to sink to her level; in *Britannicus* Agrippine manages to set the tone not only for her son but even for such as the "virtuous" Burrhus.

If evil is such a force, how is one to explain the title? Is it intentionally deceptive? Who is the tragic protagonist of the play? I am firmly convinced that the title is an easily explained anachronism by which we need neither be blinded nor bound. To those who think that the play should be called "Néron," one need only point out that no role in the play is longer or more important, or more dramatically taxing, than that of his mother, who speaks more than one-fourth of the lines. Nevertheless, it is Néron who fascinates the modern reader and viewer. But when one speaks of "tragicness," of emotions, then there is a third character involved. At every meander of this political tragedy we are made to see the lining of the cloth of politics, and at every sentence of the struggle for supremacy between mother and son we are led to ask about the one who should really be on the throne. Every time Néron or Agrippine utter the word "love," we must think of the only relatively normal love relationship in the play, that of Junie and Britannicus. The latter may not be omnipresent on stage but, like his half brother, he is ever in our minds. However, that is only part of the explanation.

Britannicus

Contemporary testimony is nearly unanimous: the public of Racine's day was quite sentimental; villains were hated and heroes cheered; exclamations interrupted many a performance, and it is said that when Narcisse told of fortune awaiting him, the murmur was such that the rest of his brief scene (II, viii) could not be heard. A look at the majority of Racine's titles shows that the titular characters are not necessarily the most flamboyant ones, but rather the ones that cause tears to be shed, or, at least, that arouse sympathy. We may center our attention on Néron; the seventeenth century loved Britannicus, as it loved Bérénice and Atalide.

It is easy to feel sympathy for Britannicus, an intelligent yet extremely naive young man who simply will not govern his behavior by what he learns about those who surround him. He confides that he is alone (323), but to Narcisse! He puts trust in Agrippine (357 sq), then regrets it bitterly somewhat later (908-14); yet he returns to her when she offers him the slightest hint of hope. Naivety in such a court can be fatal, but it is doubtful whether a shrewder Britannicus could have survived. In a world where masks govern daily life, Britannicus' pride and openly voiced ambitions concerning his rightful place do little to enhance his chances for survival. Quick to seize an opportunity, he is too inexperienced in politics to see that this can only hasten his doom: by improving his political situation, he makes his death a political necessity. In his final confrontation with his foe he drops all pretense and, with that demonstration of dash and bravura, regains an admiration he certainly had lost through his foolishness. Ironically it is his love for Junie — his only chance of happiness — that is the major cause of his undoing. His passion for Junie is not unlike that of the young lovers in *Andromaque*. At times Junie seems little more than a consolation in his bitter life (442), but he is capable of some stirring ejaculations that readily dispel this notion, as in the scene in which, under the hidden eyes of Néron, Junie tries to cool his ardor (II, vi). Of course, as was the case in *Andromaque,* it is in such scenes that he reveals this love as being self-centered, cruel, in one word, immature.

Some critics have marveled that Junie, at times so perspicacious, could love so immature a boy. But Junie herself is not devoid of naivety. It is natural that away from court she would not think it necessary to "practice deception" (641-42), but how can she fail to see the nature of life at court and be shocked, even late in the play, by the discrepancy between thought and word, or between word and deed? In a deeper sense, Néron's victory over her lies in that he does manage in the end to "pollute" her, to infect her with the vile virus that permeates his court: to survive she must pretend, don a mask. Does this not also explain her attraction for the younger Britannicus? He incorporates all the virtues, all the positive attributes of the imperial family. At times her attitude is maternal, but one may wonder whether it is the boy she loves or what he represents. She "loved" him when he was destined to reign; his very fall ties her to him (645–48).

Burrhus is perhaps the most pitiful example of the degradation that marks those who gravitate around Néron. He hates to lie (141), yet hopes to survive in a court where virtue is a handicap. He remembers his role in bringing Néron to power (857–59, 1185–86), is aware of the dubious nature of the process, yet retains a certain naivety (1325–29, 1386–89), which, coupled with an inability to act (1610, 1616–17, 1645–46), reveals him as one able to fence verbally with Agrippine or Narcisse but not to beat them at their game. Nor is he the sentimental idealist he depicts himself to be. The excuses he gives for Néron's acts (236–44), the alibis that ring false (129, 132, 235–37, 239–44, etc.), suggest self-deception rather than innocence. His very willingness to play the game dictated by Agrippine casts doubt on his integrity: how could he responsibly educate a young man who reigns because a woman killed her husband to rule through her son? How could he be true to both mother and son — or to his sense of values? The answer is readily seen at the end of act III and the beginning of the next: with Néron's threats — "Find out where my mother is ... and substitute my guard for hers" (1090–92) — still ringing in his ears, Burrhus assures Agrippine that she has probably been detained simply because her son wants to speak to her. Earlier (175–80), he had decided where his "duty" lay, with whom his lot would be cast. Politician of Rome reflecting the politics of Versailles (1331), his self-esteem is reflected in his every declaration. When Néron's true nature is finally revealed to him (III, iii), he tries to bring a modicum of moral pressure to bear, and when that fails, he seeks an alliance with Agrippine; but since he thinks of morality and she of power, it is a useless alliance whose members do not speak the same language and cannot communicate. In short, Burrhus is a politician, but a clumsy one. His ideas are good, but only in a vacuum, for he misjudges those around him and fails to act decisively when he should. Compromiser, he fails to realize that neither Agrippine nor Néron can compromise, and so is stupidly caught between the two. First believer in Néron's virtues, his eventual role is to announce the death of those virtues.

By comparison, Narcisse, his fellow mentor, is pure, though in a perverse way. In the first act he accepts the confidence of Britannicus, and nothing indicates that he is not his confidant. Only in the next act do we realize the duplicity of the man ruled exclusively by ambition (757), who is capable of anything for his advancement or his preservation.

Of all the characters in *Britannicus* only Agrippine has a confidante, and only she needs one. Junie and Britannicus have each other and Néron has his governors. Agrippine is alone, unaccepted by either the virtuous lovers or the newly self-discovered Néron. As Racine states in his preface, the play deals as much with the fall of Agrippine as with the death of her stepson or the rise of the "nascent monster." In her, that process is in reverse, as she is gradually robbed of her self-assurance. Remorseless, amoral, Agrippine has done everything for power, and she manifests neither shame nor pride as she tells how she put Claudius in her bed and Rome at her knees (1137). Nothing stopped her until "his guards, his palace, his bed" were under her control (1178), and it is no coincidence that in her tirades *bed* and *throne* are repeatedly juxtaposed. The rage and fear displayed as the play opens stem exclusively from the newly manifested freedom of her son whom — and through whom — she has ruled since the murder of her husband. As the play progresses, as she loses control over that rebellious son, she will also lose her lucidity; her moments of intuition and clairvoyance will become rarer as she endeavors to delude herself.

To keep her son under her tutelage Agrippine emphasizes the role of family ties — "He owes me, as his duty..." (20–21) — and speaks of his "unnatural" rebelliousness, the irony being that if Néron has learned to mock the sacred nature of such ties, it must have been at his mother's knees. Was it natural to murder her husband and to perpetuate her son's childhood so as to assert her own power? The very nature of her ambition — to reign, of course, but most of all to reign over Néron — is perverse. She sees his "debt" as one of love, and his rebellion becomes obvious to her when he sets his eyes on a woman whom she has not chosen for him. Viewing Junie as her rival (880) and the cause of her disgrace (879), she tries to strike back through her, but her plan is foiled by her blindness and her passion.

She never stops being a mother, however warped her maternity might be. When Néron accuses her of plotting against him because of anger and hatred (1255), he is quite right, and her protestations ring false — we *know* them to be false. Yet her possessiveness, center of that hatred, will also prevent her from carrying out her threats: she cannot bring herself to destroy that which she wants to possess. Yet her blindness is no less to blame for her downfall. Having ruled her son for so long, Agrippine cannot conceive of his having a mind of his own. When he refuses to see her, she immediately blames two of his mentors, Burrhus and Sénèque. As the situation becomes clearer — to everyone but her — Narcisse is revealed as the most influential counselor, and fear as Néron's overriding feeling vis-à-vis his mother. By the end of act III only she is unaware of the full extent of the precarious nature of her position. Nevertheless, she begins the next act with an attack on her son. How dense and foolish she appears! She can only think of how long she has waited for this interview, not of how much the situation — and her position — has changed. Not unlike the mother in *La Thébaïde,* she wants to reverse an irreversible trend and thus precipitates her downfall, making up Néron's mind. Too presumptuous (1155) to see the effects of her behavior, she never realizes that she has trained her son too well for him to remain her creature. He has been a most attentive pupil and, as Judd Hubert points out, to be truly like her, faithful to the model, he must kill her.[1]

One of Agrippine's problems is that she IS. Her thoughts, her words, are the mechanical projection of an impervious and immutable personality. What makes Néron so exciting as a dramatic character is that he is the very antithesis of that. Not yet locked into a pattern, he is totally unpredictable — though the appropriateness or "justness" of his actions and reactions may be recognized a posteriori. Néron is tired of his two years of nonreign, of three years of virtue (25, 27, 462); but the vacillation, the hesitation that we witness, is less the signal of a new birth than of an unveiling: he does not change but reveals what has been latent in him. Masking and unmasking, eyes peering from behind masks and eyes trying to see beyond masks, possessive eyes and shifty eyes — for Néron is a coward — that is what gives us some of the most spine-tingling moments of the play.

As the play opens we hear of his first move of emancipation. He still falters, asking for advice, but he seeks guidance much less than confirmation of his own choices. This is precisely the source of Narcisse's influence: whereas Burrhus, a vain man, tries to appeal to Néron's vanity (IV, iii), Narcisse readily negates that influence by telling Néron what he wants to hear. Burrhus tries to appeal to Néron's better instincts; Narcisse has only to ask Néron to remember his own desires. Both appeal to what they feel is their pupil's basic nature, and his vacillations add to the suspense, but less and less as his confidence in himself grows. However, this confidence never quite manages to eradicate his basic cowardice. Devious and arrogant, he is incapable of any true resolve before the imperious glance of his mother (505-6). This cowardice is no less obvious in his confrontations with Junie. Struck speechless in her presence, he nevertheless is excited by her purity, her rejection of him — proper goads for a man not used to rejection. Aware of his failure, Néron retreats behind a mask of urbanity. Holding Junie in his power, yet impotent, he reacts to her rejection by assuming a politeness which increases with the refinement of the mental torture he inflicts on her (II, iii); his abuse of "Madame," his précieux declarations (539-46, for example), are the least believable of his many protestations and, when they fail, are quickly discarded for a more credible brutality (619-26).[2] It is no small surprise that he tries to convert his weakness into a show of strength. When he orders Junie to be less receptive to the declarations of Britannicus, he, who cannot bear to look into her eyes, threatens her with his secret presence — he will hide while she rejects her lover, but he will watch them, hear them, scrutinize their faces — "His fate depends on you more than on me. Madam, when you see him, remember that I see you" (689-90).

For all that, Néron's passion is not primarily erotic. Burrhus is quite right when he first explains Junie's abduction as dictated by political necessity; even the murder of Britannicus can readily be seen in the same light: Britannicus is the legitimate heir — Agrippine had talked her moribund husband into disowning his son and naming Néron to the succession before she poisoned the old man — and in view of his shaky claim to the throne Néron cannot afford to neglect the possibility of a rejected Agrippine swinging her support to a pliable stepson. Were Britannicus to marry Junie, their combined claims to the imperial throne would imperil Néron's position.

At the time of the abduction Néron has never seen Junie. The love he then professes is not only sadistic and possessive, but destructive: excited and antagonized by her purity, he sees in Junie the negation of himself. As he must destroy his mother, so must he annul Junie's virtue and, in so doing, remove Britannicus' last human contact. Junie thus becomes a pawn in a sibling rivalry as well as in a struggle for power on a larger scale.³

Néron's struggle for supremacy is doomed from the start. Even when he confronts his mother with some basic truths, he feels the need to mask them. When she recites a long litany of all that she has done for him, he is only too anxious to tell her that he knows WHY and for WHOM she did it but, coward that he is, he cannot bring himself to do so openly: "...everyone is saying...that...you had worked only for yourself" (1228-30). As, earlier in the play, his face had reflected an anger (105-6) that he could not sustain before his mother, so now he capitulates to her every wish. Events will show that his capitulation only serves as a temporary buffer, that the very words he uses to acknowledge his debt of gratitude and her "power" over him are what most poisons his being, that he is "only embracing to suffocate"; but his defeat is no less established for all that.

Néron fails not only as a human being but as a tyrant. He wants to lead but is led; he wants to be free to act but can only react. Wishing to fill the shoes of Augustus, he completely misunderstands the lesson of that ancestor who saw the need to master oneself before attempting to master the universe. Like his mother, Néron wants to control people and events, but without self-control. Whereas Burrhus can make him hesitate and Narcisse can play on his fears and appetites, it is Agrippine who, by her never-dying hope to control him, by overplaying her hand, inevitably gives him the resolve he is unable to obtain on his own. Whenever Agrippine assumes a posture of power, he recoils and reacts against her.

As these characters confront each other, as they interview each other (the word is used here in its etymological sense), the masks, the alternatingly possessive and averted eyes take on a new dimension.⁴ Visually the most obvious anomaly of this play is that no one is without supervision for very long in this prison-palace. The longest monologue (III, ii) is only nine lines long, and it is ironic that half way through it Burrhus wishes there were someone present whose advice he could seek, whom he could trust. The importance of vision, of the *regard* in Racine, has not escaped the critics. In *Britannicus* it assumes for the first time proportions such that the term "voyeurism" is not excessive. Through his eyes Néron wants to observe, control, possess, and eventually, in frustration, to destroy (though it is by means of this vision that his failure to possess is brought home most vividly, that he, wishing to torture, becomes in turn tortured). This is seen in one of the most powerful lines in the play: "Madame, en le voyant, songez que je vous voi" (690);[5] Néron, having told Junie to reject Britannicus, will watch their reactions to one another. He is thus forcing her to play a charade, to become a fraud, a pathetically unsuccessful one at that. Néron is thus satisfying his most sadistic wish, but he too is unsuccessful: "Observed secretly by Néron, the eyes of Junie will no longer be able to say anything to Britannicus. By the look alone, Néron kills the exchange of looks on which subsisted the love of Junie and of Britannicus. But ... the more visible the unhappiness he provokes, the greater will be his certainty that he is not loved."[6] Junie's own interpretation of this "interview" (1002) also emphasizes the visual, and Britannicus' immediate reaction to her evasiveness is summarized in the exclamation "your eyes no longer speak, ... they fear to meet my eyes" (736-37). Néron, at that point, seems to have destroyed the mutual trust of the young lovers by preventing visual communication between them.

But has he won? From the start Néron has "disguised himself in vain" (35). He is an actor tired of a director who has manipulated him too long. Agrippine is quite frank about her activities and desires: "What do I care ... whether or not he leaves behind the model of a long virtue? Did I put him at the helm of the state so that the people and the senate could have their way?" (43-46). Néron is not escaping from virtue as much as from an insufferable tutelage. His rebellion takes the shape of an act; just as he acts the part of the précieux beau in wooing Junie, so does he act like a dutiful son and stepbrother (108-10; V, iii). This conscious parade is so ludicrous that Narcisse comments on the "spectacle [Néron] offers Rome" (1474). However, this acting is seldom successful. When Agrippine approaches the throne, she is quite aware of the reason for which Néron jumps up to greet her: "Running to embrace me, [he] kept me from the throne on which I was about to sit" (109-10).[7] The ultimate irony is not that Néron fails as an actor to convince, or as a director to fully manipulate, but that in the all-important scene in which Narcisse is killed and Junie escapes him forever, he is only an impotent spectator.

It is important to notice that this climactic scene does not take place "on stage," that is to say, in the palace. Already in *Andromaque* Racine showed a tendency to claustrophobia, as everything took place in a palace full of dark recesses and corridors, but at least that closure was broken psychologically by the possibility (Oreste, Hermione) or the desire (Andromaque) to leave it. For the first time (and by no means last) in Racine's drama, the unity of place is fully part of the action: the palace is a prison from which there is no escape. Agrippine, under house arrest, sees her own chambers turned into a prison-within-a-prison. "From the palace-trap only Junie escapes, and then only by a ruse.... Junie's escape strengthens by contrast the rôle of the palace as the site of evil: Néron, Agrippine, and the futile Burrhus remain within to fulfill the dark prophecy; Narcisse, the loathsome creature who can thrive only within the walls, meets death when he ventures without."[8]

Time, whose cyclical nature is stressed as of the first scene (32-34), is no less a part of the action. Britannicus, son of Claudius, has been removed from power through a series of deceptions and crimes. The past, then, is twofold: on the one hand, it includes virtue and great ancestry; on the other, it suggests total immorality. The opening scene not only reveals this, but also sets the stage for a desperate struggle for supremacy and survival. The criminal past has obviously perpetuated itself, becoming the present, and at stake is control of the future. Like *Andromaque*, *Britannicus* is a play torn between past and future. Between the night of the first misdeed and the night of the second a full day of light, of possible redemption unfolds. But that hope is as deceptive as Néron's greeting to his stepbrother shortly before he poisons him (1623); the obvious metaphor of day and night is flawed by the news that greets the first dawn, that of Junie's abduction (50), and the pessimistic forecast of Burrhus for the dawn that must follow the second night of crime.

The struggle during that day involves more than mother and son. The past has been brought into the present, with its glory and its gore, and — almost genetically — is incorporated in Néron. Néron, by a perverse sort of purgation, will eliminate the ancestral virtue from his being (33); Junie, on the contrary, returns to that ancestral virtue, first to the statue of Augustus (who rose above his lower instincts), then to the temple of Vesta.⁹ What at first seems like a break with the past — "The time is gone..." (91) — reveals itself with increasingly foreboding references to "that day, that sad day" (99) as a rush to doomsday (112). This crisis is a beginning, not an end. The five acts have seen the elimination in one way or another of those characters who do not belong to the reconstituted world of this perverse Caesar. We are not asked to think back in horror as much as to view this new world with even greater horror, Agrippine's occasional clairvoyance (1676) and Burrhus' final prediction exciting our imagination to "represent" Nero's Rome in most vivid detail.

Aristotle had said it; Racine repeated it in his first preface: a tragedy is "the imitation of a complete action." Yet *Britannicus* seems to begin *in medias res* and to end in such a way as to look out to a very important future. That is to confuse *history* and *action;* rather than a slice of Roman history, the tragedy is the "imitation" of a crisis. That specific crisis in which Britannicus plays a central part does not end with his death, nor does it continue after Junie's escape. As far as time is concerned, the play and the crisis coincide perfectly: one is the other. This crisis is not so much historic as psychological and moral — though moral with a twist. If realism is to be construed as a harmony with psychological verisimilitude brought to such a point that the viewer need only make a minimal effort to immerse himself in the theatrical adventure, then *Britannicus* is one of the most realistic plays ever written. Racine continues in it the shift already evident in *Andromaque,* from physical conflict to a more profound, human one. This does not mean that there are no physical elements in the play, simply that they are accessory to an inner struggle.¹⁰

On the surface Néron is unquestionably the victor. In a world that appears man-made and man-ruled, in which gods appear only by means of oblique references, Néron has imposed his new order. Yet as spectator to Narcisse's death and Junie's escape, he sees his triumphal march halted, if only temporarily. Earlier, in act III, scene viii, after a magnificent stichomythic confrontation with Britannicus, he is forced to admit defeat (1082) by having Britannicus arrested, an act that solidifies Junie's dislike for him. By his "victory," he throws the two lovers into each other's arms. As in the "spy" scene, for which Britannicus now reproaches him, he wins the battle but not the war. His constant references to what he claims to be an indifference to morality merely accentuate his awareness of moral inferiority, one that makes him lash out viciously at the next person he encounters, Agrippine. Néron wants to gain power, free himself from his mother's yoke; he kills his rival, frees himself from the mother he will murder, yet he fails. Junie escapes; but more important still, by his own attitude Néron shows that he is aware of an inner defeat. The crimes yet to come mark him as much as the ones past; worst of all the madness that we know (anachronistically, from history) is one that Néron, like Lear, may already feel coming on.

Critics have noted certain similarities between *Britannicus* and *Les Plaideurs*. In both plays a son limits the movements of a parent, even manages the life of a parent, and in both, children try to escape from parental tutelage. That much is true, but differences are more striking than similarities. Léandre manages to make an asocial father content; *Les Plaideurs* ends with the reconciliation of real and illusory worlds. *Britannicus,* unlike *Les Plaideurs* and unlike most tragedies, ends with the triumph of an illusion — not the asocial illusion of a Dandin, but the antisocial nightmare of a madman which, unlike Dandin's dream, cannot be neutralized — destined to become an infernal reality. In that sense *Britannicus* is perhaps Racine's most modern play, one which, as Marie-Odile Sweetser sees, is centered on the madness of a ruler who, like Camus' Caligula, discovers that his world is not one of pleasure and whim but simply one from which all order has been banished, one of the absurd.[11]

CHAPTER 7

Bérénice

LEGEND has it that Henrietta of England asked Racine and Corneille to write plays on the same subject, thus setting the two rivals in direct competition. This is very unlikely, and much more plausible is Raymond Picard's theory according to which *Bérénice* is Racine's challenge to a fading Corneille. The preface is still polemical, but its main thrust was aimed at the diehard critics who attacked him because only in this manner could they come out "of the obscurity to which their works condemn them." As for Corneille, Racine magnanimously contented himself with a sober defense of his own dramatic system.

According to another legend, no less unlikely than the first, *Bérénice* is a representation of the passionate love affair between Louis XIV and Marie Mancini, niece of Mazarin. This affair, perhaps the young king's only true involvement with a woman, antedated his marriage of state. Why would the usually astute Racine remind his monarch — whose favor he tried so hard to curry — of a passion that had been buried eleven years before, precisely at a time when that ruler was looking beyond the nuptial bed for erotic distractions? As the dedication graciously accepted by Colbert, the all-powerful minister, shows, Racine was a politician, not a moralist. It is quite possible that contemporaries saw obvious parallels, but it is unlikely that Racine intended to write a *pièce à clef*. The play's resounding boxoffice victory over Corneille's *Tite et Bérénice* had little to do with any possible actuality; rather Racine's tragedy best responded to the desires of a sentimental generation that was fostering the rise of lyric theater. Since then, the play has had to settle for an honorable second rank among Racine's masterpieces, well behind *Andromaque, Britannicus,* and *Phèdre*.

In the prefaces to *Alexandre* and *Britannicus* Racine had already

77

enunciated his credo of simplification. Now, in the preface to *Bérénice,* he goes further: the topic is selected precisely because of its simplicity "in the taste of the Ancients." Racine associates verisimilitude with simplicity, and inventiveness with "making something of nothing," castigating those authors whose genius does not suffice to fill five acts with "a simple action, maintained by the violence of passions, the beauty of sentiments and the elegance of expression." His play had been a huge success, tears had flown readily at every performance, and the ultimate answer to his critics is in reference to that success: "The principal rule [of drama] is to please and to touch: all the others are there only to achieve that one." *Plaire et toucher* — these then are the aims of tragedy; and how is that to be achieved? "There is no necessity for blood and death in a tragedy. It is enough that its action be great, its characters heroic, the passions aroused, and that everything exude this majestic sadness which constitutes all the pleasure of tragedy."

In keeping with this credo, the plot of *Bérénice* is extremely simple. Titus, the newly declared emperor, has just ended a week of mourning for his father Vespasien. For five years, he has been in love with Bérénice, queen of Palestine, but since a Roman ruler may not marry a foreign queen, he reluctantly decides to send her back to her "desolate Orient." Bérénice at first lashes out against the man she considers false to his vows, but eventually she appreciates his stand, and they separate by mutual consent.

The source for this play can be found in the seventh chapter of *de Tito* by Suetonius: "As for Queen Berenice, whom, it is said, he had even promised to marry, Titus sent her from the city immediately, in spite of himself, in spite of her." The full inventiveness of Racine, the extent of his ability to "make something of nothing" is best demonstrated by a less cryptic version of history. Berenice (not a queen) was born in 28 A.D.; by the time Vespasian came to quell the Judean rebellion, she had been married three times, widowed twice, and once divorced; she was thirty-eight years old. When Vespasian became emperor she was forty-one, and he sixty. Her presents pleased his greed, and her charms pleased his son Titus, his legate in Palestine, twelve years her junior. The young conqueror was handsome, cruel, and totally dissolute (as was Berenice). Having fought his father's war, Titus returned triumphantly to Rome in 71; Berenice followed him, but Vespasian immediately sent her home. In 79 Vespasian died and Titus succeeded him. Bere-

Bérénice

nice, trying to maintain a relationship that had survived on and off for twelve years, had come back to Rome, but Titus saw the danger of the situation. Renouncing his vices, he repudiated his "favorite boys" and sent Berenice away.[1]

Racine's inventiveness lies not only in the transformation of this slice of Roman history, but in the transfer of the crisis to the private sector. There are only three principal characters and three confidants;[2] Rutile, who enters twice to announce visits; Titus' attendants who appear twice, remain silent, and are dismissed after twelve lines the first time, after less than three the second; this dismissal of the only visible crowd serves to emphasize the privacy and intimacy of the action. Martin Turnell sees a fourth principal, Rome,[3] but in the climactic scenes that "outsider," like the confidants and the attendants, is excluded: it is imperative to distinguish between the will of the Senate and the will of Rome, as one must distinguish between the law and the spirit of the law to which Bérénice is sacrificed. Furthermore, public pressure merely sets the machinery in motion; the eventual decision must come from within the trio. It is most interesting to see how that final scene is set. In the antepenultimate scene Titus and Bérénice debate in the presence of her mute confidante who is then dismissed to seek Antiochus; in the penultimate scene the two lovers are alone, but cannot reach agreement or find a solution. "Two may be a couple," but it is not a couple that is sought here, it is a tableau, an idealization of love, and, as we shall see shortly, Antiochus is needed as a catalyst before Bérénice can say "Let us all three serve as examples to the universe" (1502). No messenger need announce an event; no confidant need comment. The tension derives from the trio and must be resolved by it alone.

Bérénice, frequently called the "most Racinian play," is in many ways also a most Cornelian one. As in *Le Cid,* the lovers surrender temporal joy for the sake of their love. Dominance over the physicality of love makes *Bérénice,* like *Le Cid,* a tragedy of deliberate personal sacrifice. As in *Le Cid,* the characters of *Bérénice* assume a role in search of a destiny, a place in history. Awakening to the obligations that this assumption entails, they sublimate all human feelings to that new *Weltanschauung,* but this in no way eliminates these feelings. The individual is sacrificed to the role, and the tragic emotion derives from our awareness of the characters' own consciousness of the reasons, nature, and effects of the immolation. As long as Titus merely gropes for a truth, for an all too obvious solution based on rationalization, he evokes scorn rather than pity. Once he fully realizes *why* his original decision was the right one, he becomes truly tragic. He cannot do this alone, and it cannot come from the many scenes of hesitation and diatribe; it does come finally when the three lovers forget their selfish motives and reveal each other to themselves and to one another.[4]

As in *Britannicus,* the titular character is the one for whom tears are shed, but the impetus for the action comes from another direction. The rise of Titus to power contains a first irony. As a prince he could behave as he pleased (458); as emperor he can make or break kings (721) but cannot dispose of his own heart. He offers lands to the woman who wants only his love; separated from life by a newly acquired sense of duty — *vivre* and *régner* are juxtaposed throughout the play — his gifts mean exile and death to her. This is not the result of a blinding revelation, a secular grace as some would have it.[5] He has known all along that Roman law forbade the union he most desired, but he preferred to ignore that truth (1088-90). This knowledge, the "obstacles," arouses him even more, as Bérénice remarks, but now there is a new imperative, *noblesse oblige.* As emperor he must view things with the eyes of an emperor (1098).

It is also ironic that it was Bérénice who urged Titus on to develop his full potential. He agreed to be worthy of her, to put her on the throne. Now her travails bear their bitter fruit (519-23). Idol of Rome, he must live up to his reintegrated generosity by rejecting Bérénice.

Despite this, Titus is at first undecided (1225-26). His love is voiced throughout the play, and Bérénice, some cruel taunts notwithstanding, believes him (1500). It preoccupies him even in the senate, but indecision marks his words whenever he is in the presence of the beloved (1382). And yet it bears repeating that the play does not hinge on whether or not Titus knows his duty, but on whether he will have the strength to resist temptation and live by his decision. He knows that he must reign rather than live: "Mais il ne s'agit plus de vivre, il faut régner" (1102). In that important line the sixth beat comes on *plus* ("no longer"), directly juxtaposing in the second hemistich the two verbs "live" and "reign." During these moments of indecision the role of Paulin, his confidant, deserves comment. Paulin is not merely Roman, as his use of

Bérénice

possessives shows (409-19): he is Rome. To him the "Orient" is a voluptuous trap and his references to Cleopatra — historically inaccurate — are obviously meant as warnings, not precedents that might legitimize a union with Bérénice. As he says, no one, not even Nero who broke so many laws, dared break that one (387-93). This thorough Roman, however close a friend he might be, has no understanding of Titus' love (422, 516) and so, having become superfluous — or useless — he drops out of sight before the last act.

Paulin, with all his shortsightedness, is quite right: Titus cannot belie his innate virtues, his generosity (491-98). Titus is aware of this: "And only I could destroy myself" (1087). Only he can safeguard his desire to be exemplary, and, as John Lapp has put it, that desire is not "overweening self-satisfaction." When Bérénice finally understands this, she echoes "Titus' frequently reiterated expression of responsibility to a universe which in a geographical and historical sense looks upon his every move for guidance."[6]

Whereas Titus is torn — "Ah, Rome! Ah, Bérénice!" (1225) — Bérénice knows only her love for which she is willing to sacrifice everything: "One sigh, one glance, one word from your lips, that is the ambition of a heart such as mine" (576-77). That is why, until the last thirty-six lines, she understands neither the duty of a good ruler nor that of a good lover. She thinks that a ruler can do as he pleases, that a lover, to be happy, need only surrender to the pleasures of love. Open and frank she has "a care to please without artifice" as Titus puts it (543), and that is precisely what prevents her from understanding and makes her so unfair (1147, 1175, etc.): in Titus' hesitations she senses betrayal. It is therefore doubly ironic that every time Titus comes to her in indecision he leaves resolved to be himself, in spite of himself, in spite of her.

Self-centered Bérénice is not only unfair in her confrontations with Titus, she is needlessly cruel to poor Antiochus to whose passion she remains completely insensitive (e.g., I, iv). Such is her arrogant rebuke of the unfortunate king that her own confidante, Phénice, feels obliged to rebuke her. That scene is doubly interesting. Firstly because we are made aware of Bérénice's egoism and egotism; secondly because Phénice does not stick to the sentimental issue. She feels that her mistress is burning too many bridges; Rome hates foreigners; if Titus were to reject her, she might rue her harsh treatment of Antiochus. Eventually we will see that she is right in her own pedestrian way (with that same retrospective knowledge we will know that Bérénice was also right not to settle for the compromise that is Antiochus). In short, Phénice posits the level at which things had been happening and might continue to happen in a melodrama. The level at which she thinks indicates what will have to be transcended in tragedy.[7]

Bérénice's pride is apparent in her rejection of Antiochus. It is no less so in her reactions to the Roman mob. After Caesar's death Cleopatra had left Rome because she sensed its scorn. Bérénice, as aware of *gloire* as Titus, is afraid of an analogous fate (1179). She knows that the people are fickle, that the senate may approve of her today and change its mind tomorrow, and it is with little surprise that she describes the "insulting mob" which only a short time before flocked around her and now howls with "cruel joy" at her misfortune (1313-15). This might be considered the beginning of the awakening of the proud queen. Eventually she comes to realize that Titus is giving her the greatest possible proof of love, and it is that realization, precipitated by Antiochus' threat of suicide, that leads to her "redemption," her erotic apotheosis.

The word is not too strong. To be sure the impetus has come from Titus and Antiochus, but she has gone beyond. Titus has made a choice between life and the throne. She now sees that such a duality is superficial. "I shall live," she says (1493), and tells Antiochus to do likewise (1498). This new life will be a rejection of the half-measures, the escapes into suicide offered by the men who speak only of "turmoil, horrors, blood about to flow" (1474). What she offers is the only worthy "example" (1502), one of transcendence and transfiguration. In this magnificent gesture Bérénice "no longer thinks of glory, she gives herself entirely to a last celebration of their love." It is not the sacrifice but the love that becomes exemplary and legendary.[8]

What of the unfortunate lover left behind by this transfigured couple? Antiochus has suffered longer than they: silent for five years he has accepted not to be himself, and as Titus and Bérénice treat him as an insensate witness, not to have — or at least not to voice — any feelings. Though he frequently wallows in self-pity, he consistently shows himself to be the epitome of self-sacrifice, even becoming the *porte-parole* of his rival, though he remains more in love than ever (258).[9] Not until the last scene does he fully assert himself by suggesting a suicide that is not a surrender to self-pity, but a rational (1456) sacrifice (1468). Wrenching himself free of his long passivity he not only opens Bérénice's eyes, but demands what is rightfully his: a place in the final tableau that will serve as an example to history. Believing Titus and Bérénice reconciled, he will kill himself to assure their happiness, as an offering to the gods, to appease them. It is this selfless sacrifice that shows Bérénice what an unselfish love can do, what it must do. She now understands the two men, what they have done, and what she must do. The irony, of course, is that Antiochus has done the right thing for the wrong reason: the two lovers are not reconciled and, if anything, his grandiose speech crystallizes their separation.

Antiochus is a good man, but like Don Sanche in Corneille's *Cid,* he is merely second best. Titus "came, saw, and pleased" Bérénice (194). Here, as in *Le Cid,* the heart instinctively recognized eventual superiority. As Chimène's father had said of her two lovers, "Both are worthy of her"; but Chimène's heart had sensed immediately that the equality was a mere illusion, that Rodrigue, the future "Cid," was the better man. Bérénice saw in Titus a future emperor, virtuous and generous enough to — irony of ironies! — reject her. At the end of the play, all three characters will prove exemplary, but Antiochus' parting "Alas" shows that his sacrifice is a most reluctant one; once again he has been good, but not quite good enough, and in the final analysis he is still alone.

As it must be obvious from the foregoing, there is no question of obeying the rules governing the three unities which are part and parcel of the essence of this drama, since, being purely psychological, it has no reason to expand. What few peripeteias there are, are necessary to show the hesitations of a hero on the brink of failing himself (1087). This "most Racinian play," stands out as Racine's only tragedy (with the possible exception of *Alexandre*) in which the protagonists are not crushed by destiny but called by destiny to find in themselves the mettle to rise above all contingencies. The final sacrifice of the three lovers is not only conscious and lucid, but voluntary;[10] the entire play is centered on the communication of an awareness and a will. This is a painful process, and while the protagonists frequently seek each other out to fathom each other and themselves, they avoid each other with equal frequency. Critics have at times objected to what they considered a structural weakness, a momentarily empty stage, as after act IV, scene ii. Bérénice has been alone with Phénice; Titus approaches with a large retinue;

since Bérénice is seeking a tête-à-tête, she withdraws before the crowd, symbol of intrusion. We have heard her side of the problem; now Titus dismisses everyone and alone bursts forth in exalted lyricism (IV, iv). Only then are we ready for the climactic scene of confrontation (IV, v). Though Bérénice will not understand everything until the last thirty-six lines of the lay, this scene is essential to the dramatic and psychological progression of the action, and nothing prepares us for it as well as that scenic "rupture" earlier in the act.[11]

The locus of this drama is simultaneously more restricted and vaster than that of any previous play. As the first lines of the play indicate, the curtain rises on a private cabinet of unusual loftiness of design and conception. It is a "proud and isolated" room in which the emperor seeks refuge from Roman intrusion. Two of its doors lead to the chambers of Titus and of Bérénice. These doors are closed as the curtain rises; when it drops five acts later, will they not close "for a last time" (1506)? It is a small yet pompous place, proper setting for a private yet regal tragedy. However, it is not the *huis-clos* of *Britannicus*. Antiochus is anxious to leave it, and only a temporary restraint by Titus (a friendly request, not an ominous order) keeps him at hand. What Bérénice fears most is not to be locked in, but to be locked out, exiled to "l'Orient désert." In this play *exil* and *désert* are not a matter of geography but of personal presence or absence. The Orient became a desert to Antiochus only when Bérénice left it for Rome. Once Bérénice leaves Rome, Titus will be "more exiled than she" (752), and his reign "will be a long banishment" (754). Thus, as each lover goes into a separate exile, one without end or self-delusion (798, 918), the locus loses its limits with its function.

Much the same can be said of the element of time. The past and future play a greater role than in earlier Racine plays, yet the tragedy is precisely situated in a restricted "now". Since Bérénice is finally receiving her admirers, we may suppose that, according to mundane practices of the seventeenth century, the play begins in the afternoon; it flows smoothly, with minimal time lapses between acts: a few minutes between acts I and II, not over an hour during the other intermissions; from opening to closing curtain one may safely suppose a "real" time lapse of not over five hours. Since Vespasian died June 22, 79, since a week of mourning followed, and since the play takes place the day after the end of that mourning ("for eight days"), it is certain that *Bérénice* represents events that took place on June 30, 79 A.D. This little chronological game is intended only to emphasize the circumscription of time and to put in relief what follows.[12]

In *Bérénice,* as in most Racinian plays, the past comes to bear on the present, but this play is different in that time is exploded and the past funneled into the momentary present, which is then lengthened into hours not only to heighten the tension, but also to focus our attention — and sympathy — on the eternity of sorrow to follow. It is this very process which bears scrutiny.

Basically, there are four distinct "time blocks" in *Bérénice:* the five years that have elapsed since the first meeting of Titus and Bérénice; the week of mourning; the present; the future. Each one of these is endowed with a very particular aura and a vocabulary to match.

The love affair of Titus and Bérénice has lasted for five years, but this must not be construed as a monolithic entity: "For five whole years I have seen her every day" (545),[13] says Titus, and each subsequent reference to that time reemphasizes that for the lovers every day, every encounter, was a new and welcome discovery. For Titus each one of these five years was made up of consecutive days, every one of which was a new opportunity "to see her..., love her, please her" (424), or rather to fall in love with her all over again (545-46). These five years are the sum total of a love, but of a love that is constituted by a series of happy moments each one of which, though an echo of the previous one, retains its freshness and individuality. That these five years are to be counted day by day is made even more obvious by a count of the actual words used to describe them: the words *an, ans, année,* and *années* occur only ten times in the entire play, whereas *jour, jours, journée,* and *journées* occur nearly fifty times. Referring to that period of time Antiochus, in 1671, was made to say, "But since after five years I dare to speak out" (206). In later editions Racine changed this to, "But since at this moment...." The change of focus from the past five years to this pressing moment is obvious.

Between those five years and "this moment" the world of Titus and Bérénice has come to a standstill. No personal decision can be made until Rome has reached a public one. For eight days Titus has reigned, but he has been totally inactive. These days have been "an austere retreat" (55). As he admits, "I have reigned for eight days," but "what account can I give of so precious a time?" (1029-31). "Twenty times" (473) in those eight days he has tried to communicate with Bérénice, but each time words have failed him. His silence — "My mouth and eyes, silent for eight days" (737) — has added to the tension and to the feeling of impending disaster. These eight days, then, of separation and suspense, *are* monolithic, a single void whose main purpose is to lead to "this moment" and to set its mood.

After that period of "long" love (150) and of the "long mourning" (153) that has "suspended" that love (154) comes the time for decision. This is not *some* time, but *the* moment. The word "moment," singular or plural, occurs thirty-nine times in *Bérénice,* eleven times in the first act alone.[14] In all but three of these instances there is no doubt: "this moment" is "the moment" (22, 29, 67, etc.). It is easy to schematize the time elements involved into an inverted pyramid having a broad base of five years and its entire weight resting on the single point of focus, "this very moment," as Bérénice calls it (318). By the same token it might be said that this point is also the apex of another pyramid, one extending into an eternity entirely derived from this momentous occasion.

"Now is the time," says Paulin late in the second act (556). This remark is noteworthy only because the fact has been obvious for some time now (1, 21-22, 29, 67, 72-73, 125, etc.), and because it makes it obvious that the question of whether we have "one moment" or are going "from moments to moments" (73), is the reason for this procrastination. When Paulin reminds us that it is indeed time, suspense has already reached a certain pitch. Yet Racine keeps on raising it. Entire acts are tied together by the feeling of expectation honed by the author. At the end of act I Bérénice announces an "interview" which will allow "feelings long held in check" (326) to be released. This procedure is repeated at the end of each act, with an echo taking up the theme at the beginning of the next one, so that by the beginning of act IV, when Bérénice fretfully asks herself why Phénice has not yet come bearing glad tidings, it has contributed at least as much as the peripeteias to the establishment of an unbearable suspense. In other words, "this moment" has been exploded into still smaller components by means of delaying maneuvers and, more effective yet, by the hiatuses between maneuvers.

At the beginning of the play "that moment" and all the subsequent moments are viewed quite differently by the various protagonists. Most striking are the diametrically opposed views of Bérénice and Antiochus. To him the now is merely a "last time," the last chance to utter "a final farewell" (178). Early in the play he uses "last time" most frequently, whereas Bérénice speaks more often of "first time." Her optimistic view of the future emphasizes the pessimism of the neglected Antiochus. But little by little as delay follows delay, her outlook changes, and she comes to view her future under a different light: how will she be able to stand dawn and dusk without him (1115), what indeed will "these days so long" (1121) hold in store for her? No longer can she view the present as the beginning of a uniformly happy future. Rather, as the truth dawns on her, she realizes that this future, like the five years gone by, will be made up of individual days, but this time empty (1117) and without hope. Love, in that ever-recurring day, will have to exist without daily proof, and it is this realization that makes the ultimate "for the last time" so searing: the last contact will now be replaced by the first of many absences. There will be no single, dull ache, but the daily renewal of acute realization and pain.

The present in *Bérénice* is the continuation of the past: it is also its ending, its culmination. Eventually Titus (1292), Antiochus (1454), and Bérénice (1506) admit that there comes a time when repetition or delay must cease, when for all things good or bad there has to be "a last time." The present then is the end of the past; it is also the door to the future. It is, so to speak, a hinge between past experience and the future realization of a higher state. This is made obvious in act III, scene i, when Titus, taking leave of Antiochus, defines Bérénice as "all that was my heart's sole desire, all that I will love to my dying breath" (769-70). This shift in focus is restated by Bérénice in the final scene: "For five years, to this day, I believe to have given you assurances of a true love. That is not all; on this fateful day, I wish to crown the rest with a last effort: I shall live, I shall obey your absolute orders. Farewell, my lord, reign: I shall not see you again" (1489-94). At that sublime and tragic moment Bérénice abandons all dreams of happiness and resolutely faces a lifetime of sorrow, one all the more awesome in its bleakness in that every one of its empty moments will be a painful reminder of the past. In both instances, by changing the focus from past experience to future commitment, Titus and Bérénice have shifted from all the contingencies of the physical world to the safety of immutable feelings which they have, by that single shift in focus, endowed with a reality more vivid than any physical one could be.

CHAPTER 8

Bajazet

HAVING proved that the majestic sadness of tragedy could be evoked without bloodshed, the "tender" Racine now showed his ferocious side. Not only is blood readily spilled in *Bajazet,* but the tormentors reveal a sadism which surpasses that of Néron. Like *Britannicus, Bajazet* is a metaphorical hell located in a palace-as-prison, a tight enclosure reeking of doom. The cruelty, deceit, and violence that pervade this seraglio are less a representation of the Ottoman Empire than the picture that Racine's contemporaries had of it.

Murad IV, "the Cruel," was born in 1609 and ruled from 1623 to 1640, with his mother as regent until 1632. In 1635, at the time of the first campaign against the Persians, he followed the dynastic custom of ridding himself of rivals by having two of his three surviving brothers, Bayezid and Suleiman, killed (the third, Ibrahim, was mentally retarded and not considered a rival; allowed to live, he eventually succeeded Murad). The last of his dynasty to personally lead his troops to war, he took Baghdad (Babylon in the play) in 1638 and had all its inhabitants massacred. He quelled the Janissaries' rebellion, purged the state of corrupt officials, and eventually died of what must be considered the results of sexual overexertion.

Much of this was known to Racine through the French ambassador to Turkey, but only indirectly — despite his prefatorial protestations, he probably never met the ambassador. Many books existed on the Ottoman Empire, and he undoubtedly had read these, as he must have read or seen plays such as Mairet's *Soliman* or Tristan's *Osman.* When *Bajazet* was first performed in January, 1672, Corneille's partisans, stung undoubtedly by its success, complained that the play was not Turkish, that it was a French costume play and an inaccurate one at that. In his preface Racine countered by claiming that he had been most faithful to the mores and customs of Turkey, but he, like his adversaries, was overstating the case: the local color of *Bajazet* is psychological, sacrificing verity to verisimilitude.

While Sultan Amurat is trying to conquer Babylon, the Grand Vizier Acomat is in charge of the city, and the Sultan's favorite, Roxane, with full powers over the seraglio, has received orders to execute Bajazet, Amurat's brother. Feeling his favor slipping, Acomat has decided to foment a palace revolt by encouraging a liaison between Bajazet and Roxane; Acomat himself covets Atalide, princess of royal blood, but only for the power she can bring him. Acomat and Roxane use Atalide as intermediary for the Roxane-Bajazet liaison, unaware of the fact that Atalide and Bajazet love one another. While everyone wonders as to the success of Amurat and the effect of his fortunes on the various domestic plots, his slave Orcan is sent to hasten Bajazet's death. Roxane offers Bajazet his life if he will marry her and have Atalide killed before his eyes; when he refuses, she has him strangled, but too late: Orcan executes his orders to kill the unfaithful favorite. Orcan is massacred in turn as Atalide kills herself on the body of her beloved and Acomat escapes to a boat he has kept in readiness.

As Raymond Picard puts it, "In no other tragedy, perhaps, are the political and erotic intrigues so abominably intertwined,"[1] each level absurd from the viewpoint of the other. To Acomat, love is only a political instrument, as he manipulates human beings and human hearts to suit his ambition. Roxane constantly reminds her prisoner of her power in order to subdue his rebellious heart. "Atalide and Bajazet love each other, but the political conditions forbid the realization of that love: they have the love, but not the power: Roxane, on the other hand, has the power, but no love," says Picard who sees three "fatalities": love, politics, and the Sultan's vengeance. All the characters in this play are phantoms fighting a battle that is beyond their capabilities, for, in the eyes of the master, they are all as good as dead.[2] In a play replete with ironies, the biggest irony of all lies in the general misunderstanding of the Sultan's "presence" which threatens Roxane no less than Bajazet. What all these schemers fail to realize is that there is no perfect moment to take advantage of the master's absence: his power is still as much in the seraglio as in Babylon. In no other play of Racine do so many people have such faith in their power to act, to affect their destiny; and no play equals *Bajazet* for its resounding answer to that illusory feeling of autonomy from an imposed fate.

The characters *seem* to have a certain power, as Amurat *seems* unaware of rules of state whch dictate that a ruler should be present to be effective. As Hobbes and Machiavelli state, will and power are nil if the holder is absent. But has Amurat really left? Has his power really been delegated to what Bajazet calls a "selfish slave?" Amurat and the Janissaries (who killed his half brother Osman) had an uneasy relationship of mutual hatred, fear, and mistrust. To take them into the field to a probable victory is a calculated risk which, as events show, assured their support and his supremacy. As events also demonstrate, once the Janissaries are won over, the harem intrigue becomes a minor matter to be readily resolved. Amurat returns not only as supreme commander of his soldiers, but rid of a rebellious vizier, a rival brother, and a very unreliable "favorite."

In one respect all the characters of *Bajazet* are lucid: they are all conscious of the diverse feelings that move them. What they do not know are the feelings and motives of their protagonists, or the state of things in the broader sense, and in this drama of lies and deceit in which the truth can kill — and does, namely, Atalide — ignorance is bliss. Ironically, it is Atalide, so ready to deceive, who first proves incapable of sustaining the deadly game and, by her revelation, precipitates the bloody climax. Ibrahim the imbecile is safe only because he is considered inoffensive. As long as Roxane remains ignorant of the Bajazet-Atalide relationship, she is happy. Lucidity is deadly in a situation where, as Judd Hubert points out, *exposer* has always two simultaneous meanings, "to reveal" and to "expose to danger."[3] Under these circumstances normal relationships are meaningless. Bajazet and Atalide are of royal blood, Roxane a slave; yet the latter is seemingly omnipotent while Atalide is treated like a handmaiden. Bajazet, under sentence of death, is constantly made aware of his inferiority. Roxane uses the polite *vous* when she wishes to cajole, but anger makes her quickly lapse into the more familiar *tu*. Reminding Bajazet that she has spared him and can kill him (524; "Go back to the void whence I drew you") she forces him to acknowledge her omnipotence: "Ma vie est votre bien" (519; "My life is your property"). To her he is indeed little more than an object, a piece of property.

As Roxane will eventually discover, her power, like that of Acomat, is an "illusion comique," a theatrical illusion adroitly staged by the "absent" Amurat. While the supposedly wise and wily Acomat is constantly misinformed by false reports and by his flawed sense of observation, Roxane is betrayed by her blinding passions. The deception of Acomat begins in the first scene with both reader and spectator taken in: Acomat and his confidant trade information in what *seems* like a perfect expository scene. Only later do we discover that their far from neutral vision was flawed, that when Acomat stated that Bajazet and Roxane had "bound forever their hearts and fortunes" (162), he was not reporting a fact, but indulging in wishful thinking. As the denouement reveals, only one person seems to know throughout what is really happening; only one person therefore has a proper basis for action — and therefore true power — and that is Amurat; all the others are merely players unconscious of the comic illusion being perpetrated, thinking that they have control over their destiny or that of others. By the same token, whereas every character in the play seeks freedom from Amurat, only he — who resented the "tutelage" (42) of the Janissaries whom he feared as much as they feared him (44) — is eventually emancipated.

As in *Britannicus,* the theme of emancipation from an unwanted tutelage is stated early in the play, but here the palace is a prison for all the protagonists. There are almost no references to the outside world; Babylon is mentioned a few times, but only in connection with Amurat and his decisive battle, and if allusion is occasionally made to the sea as a road of escape, that same sea awaits the bodies of all those who defy the powers that be (30). In this enclosure Roxane rules a world of slaves and mutes who have sold their "servile souls" for the sake of survival (434–37). Acomat and Osmin, embittered soldiers, are outsiders in such a realm, whatever their political acumen may be. Two of the confidants are listed as slaves, but are Bajazet, Atalide, and Roxane much more than that? The first two are at the mercy of the third who, when all is said and done, is also a de facto slave. The delegation of authority (from Amurat) serves more to emphasize dependency than power. "Let the seraglio be closed and everything return to the accustomed order" (571–72). Roxane's threat is also a statement of resignation to the inevitable. The rhymes of *fermé* and *order accoutumé* are most interesting: slavery is the norm in this palace. Acomat is to leave and then, having recognized Amurat's sovereignty, Roxane will shut the gates, resigned to regaining her slave's status. Eventually, like Bajazet, she will even die at the hands of a slave.

In this enclosure time is as limited as space. Racine realized that his public, though familiar with Greek and Roman mythology, was relatively ignorant of recent Turkish history. Rather than diffuse that history throughout the play, he chose an approach that would make it superfluous. The past is unimportant, its effects few and immediate, centered mostly on Amurat's orders. As for the future, it does not exist. There is only the present, "this day" (318), "this very moment" (321). The constant looks to the future are couched in irony, for there is no future: it is destroyed with the protagonists in the "final holocaust."[4] But this is no *Bérénice,* and time is neither frozen nor exploded. There is rather a sense of "pitiless urgency,"[5] of constant acceleration to the very end. Time is precious, hesitation fatal. On this "precious day" (1332), only moments "too precious to be wasted on words" (1470) count for anything. Yet it is words that have started the rebellion: Acomat has spoken to Roxane (135-38), and his words have made her want to meet Bajazet. It is the false rumor of Amurat's death that is amplified verbally by Roxane to give her an excuse to meet Bajazet (147-48). It is through words that Acomat brings the two together, and it is Bajazet's refusal to utter the proper words that dissolves the triumvirate which might have replaced Amurat.[6]

Racing to their doom — Acomat survives, but only as a ruined man — these gallicized Turks present themselves as some of the most problematic of Racine's characters: strange hybrids uniting heroic and despicable traits, they are at times attractive, frequently repulsive, and always interesting, provided an effort is made to keep their particular *race, moment,* and *milieu* in mind.

Like his shadow Osmin, Acomat is an embittered soldier; both have been recently slighted by Amurat, and they fear worse (86-91), but their rebellious machinations make it difficult to see them as slighted worthies. Acomat sees only the effects of things. Proud of his amoral conduct and lack of sentimentality, he advises Bajazet to do anything to succeed, even to break vows (642-50) as his ancestors had frequently done, considering a vow as a tool, not an obligation. Yet this man, who can so clearly analyze political situations, who is a master of the art of intrigue, wallows in a feeling of superiority that is simply groundless: impervious to feelings, he cannot properly assess those of others; without a grasp of the nature and importance of human emotions, he constantly misinterprets the words and gestures of the people he manipulates. He trusts only his own daring and knowledge of court intrigue (1389-94), but it is obvious that this old soldier knows more about the theory of intrigue than its practice, and he owes his life ultimately only to the foresight which made him keep his boats in readiness for a possible escape. He is, in every way, the "outsider."

If one expects the titular character of a play to be endowed with epic virtues, it is only too easy to be disappointed with Bajazet. In his earlier days he may have been a brave warrior, but he is now a disinherited prince under sentence of death. Cloistered in the seraglio, surrounded by mutes and eunuchs, his spirits have been if not broken, at least warped. Viewed in that light, his defects — ingredients of his humanity — are forgivable. Nor is his role the largest (each of the women has nearly twice as many lines as he) or the most dynamic. Ill at ease in the atmosphere of intrigue, he knows that his fate — constantly debated by others — depends on his decision to say what Roxane wants to hear. As far as the latter is concerned, Bajazet is a thing that will be done unto, not an active participant in the debate. Yet despite these two attitudes, the central moral crisis is his. Most of the play centers around his decision to be honest, regardless of cost. He does have a conscience, and the haunting question is what it will take to make it speak up.

Bajazet is a complex personality. A valiant soldier from his earliest years, he dies a soldier's death, since he slaughters many of his would-be killers (1700) before succumbing to their numbers. But between these two periods of glory is one of survival at any cost which has left its stain of cynicism and fatalities. "Roxane saw the prince; ... Bajazet is lovable [who arouses love]; he saw that his salvation depended on his pleasing her, and soon he pleased her" (153-56). In that marvelous example of preterition Acomat presents the Bajazet of the seraglio, the prince willing to prostitute himself to save his life.

Nowhere is this aspect of his personality more evident than in the opening scene of the second act. Roxane has proposed marriage as a sine qua non of his survival. He has neither the courage nor the rectitude to tell her his true feelings: he is in love with Atalide, and he considers Roxane nothing more than a selfish slave (718-19); she considers his rejection of her a betrayal, but he considers acquiescence a double betrayal, of love and honor. Instead of stating the true reasons for his refusal, he blames his lack of stature, the tradition of regal celibacy, and finally tries to win her over by presenting a faint ray of hope — "Perhaps in time, ... first put me in a position to reward you..." (494-96) — though he knows very well that he would never marry her. Her ironic reply hits like a slap: spurred on by her love, she has been too prompt; his "foresight" makes him aware of all the dangers that her proposed course would bring to bear on his honor. She then calls on the only argument he seems willing to understand: "But have you foreseen, if you don't marry me, the even more certain dangers that you run?" (497-504). The next nine lines contain as many questions, all restatements of the same idea: never forget that I am mistress of your fate. His clumsy and ineffective answer deals with an acknowledged debt, but with such reticence that the woman who had been able to halt Amurat's polygamy explodes in anger, defeated by the slippery Bajazet. She makes one last attempt, an open declaration of passion, and when that is rejected, she admits defeat, sending Bajazet to his apparent doom. This scene will be repeated twice (III, v; V, iv), and only in the last one does Bajazet change from ambiguous reticence to outraged rejection. His only firm stand is due to a reaction of revulsion rather than a decision of righteousness.

Bajazet speaks of his ancestral valor (738-40), of his rectitude; he sees himself as vehemently opposed to lies, and Atalide readily agrees (1592), but he shows little of that rectitude during the play and ultimately must recognize that though he did not utter a lie, he allowed one to be formulated, encouraging Roxane's misconception. Not only are his words equivocal, so are his gestures, and Acomat, watching from afar, misinterprets his "eloquent glances" as readily as Roxane (887-88).[7] His perennial defense, that he has merely been silent, is a weak one. Atalide admits no less in her apostrophe to her ancestors, calling them "Heroes who were to relive in this hero" (1740). The tense *(deviez revivre)* is most important: not "who *did* live," but "who were supposed to live." She knows that Bajazet did not fulfill his potential and bemoans the loss of what could have been, not of what was.

Atalide, the play's only true lover, does not condemn Bajazet's deception, but she laments the destruction of an essence. Hers is a strange role. Since it was originally given to the famous Champmeslé, we know that Racine did not intend to see Roxane dominate the stage with her unrelenting savagery. Like Antoine Adam[8] I am tempted to think that Racine wanted to put into each play someone who would console him (and us) for all the surrounding evil. Not that Atalide is the pure princess, the innocent and pitiful victim of Roxane. Like Bajazet she hates deception (353) but feels that circumstances necessitate it for the preservation of her love and her lover's life (354-56). In this stultifying climate the unfortunate couple has had to learn to love in secret (366: "nous aimer et nous taire"). Roxane, by the danger she presents as well as by her credulity, has encouraged the lovers' deception (374-76).

Atalide lives only for her love, without the ambition of Bajazet or the cruel possessiveness of Roxane. Such is that love that despite her jealousy — at times she claims that she would rather see Bajazet dead than in Roxane's arms (682-86) — she is able and willing to step aside to save his life (400, 836). Knowing that he is willing to die is enough for her: she orders him to live (708), and repeatedly reminds herself of that order. When Bajazet triumphantly announces that he has obeyed, she considers her life at an end (959), particularly since she believes him to be incapable of treachery (391) and therefore now truly in love with Roxane (963-68). Ironically, by her inability to carry through in a duel of artifice with Roxane, she unveils his deception and thus causes his death. Basically, both Bajazet and Atalide are unwilling and ineffective schemers; their sophistry cannot eradicate their *artifice* and *feintes*. The supreme irony lies not in their death (Bajazet is doomed by his birth, not his deeds), but in their moral decay; they prostituted themselves in vain — it did not save them.

More than Bajazet, more than Atalide, Roxane is the product of the harem, a woman ruled exclusively by her senses and her appetites, magnificent in her fury, despicable in her vices, touching in her frustration. Racine gave the role of Atalide to the star, for the seventeenth-century public wanted to be *touché;* neither critics nor performers leave any doubt that today the great role of *Bajazet* is considered to be that of Roxane, a most difficult one, for, as so many critics have noted, it is a dual one: within whose lines an insecure lover fights a ruler imbued with a false sense of security. Whenever the sultana threatens, the lover voices apprehension and foresees regrets.

In the very first line of the play Roxane is called "sultana," but the validity of that title is one of the crucial questions of the drama. Amurat has given her the title, he has put her in charge of the seraglio, but he has refused to marry her; she is merely the favorite in a large harem whose power, as I have already stated, is in large part imaginary. She owed her rank and position exclusively to her looks and her ability to charm and seduce. Now she wants Bajazet, in part to escape from Amurat's threatening presence,[9] but no less "to clothe herself in the purity, stature, and legitimacy which an official marriage with Bajazet would afford."[10]

Roxane, feared by her slaves, is far from free herself, being constantly watched by seraglio guards whose attention she must circumvent by subterfuge. The emperor is absent, but a crowd of slaves represents his presence and his wishes, the "ordre accoutumé." Not only do these slaves have a price, but so does Roxane and the man she loves. "If he could only save himself at that price," says Zaïre (812). Atalide, who is the "prize" promised Acomat (854), knows that Roxane's good graces have a price (866) and so does Bajazet (1031), long before Roxane reminds him in bluntest terms (1547). In a den of slaves the price tag tells the worth of a human being, and the equation marks all relationships, including love.

This in part explains how Roxane can think of threatening Bajazet while expressing her "love," which is the only reason he has survived so far (505-12). As Bajazet recognizes (519), she considers him as a possession. What is more, she views his love in the same vein, and when he responds to her threats by pledging mere gratitude and respect, her frustration and anger are unleashed.[11] Though she cannot control her heart (1085), she fully expects to control that of others.

Roxane's thirst for power, for honor and respectability, is neutralized by her genuine (though warped) passion for the prince. Torn between the two she constantly changes her mind as she wavers between lucidity and blindness, between unreasoned optimism and awareness of her "weakness" (553).[12] Long before she realizes that Bajazet does not love her, Roxane is dismayed by his hesitations. She who rose to power by capturing the heart of a polygamous sultan, who knew how to make herself supremely loved, senses failure. Her hesitation — "Which is my emperor??" (1115) — fully shows her vulnerability. Ever insecure, ever suffering, she hides behind a cruel mask of deception and irony. Her lies, unlike those of Atalide — not too unlike those of Bajazet — are poker-faced double-entendres and equivocal answers. To these she adds a purely personal dimension of ironic understatement, as when she tells her rival that she "cannot hate" Bajazet (1199). This aspect can also reveal her sadistic side as when, having sent Bajazet to his death, she torments Atalide, who is unaware of the latest developments, with the assurance: "Far from separating you, I intend this very day to unite you two by eternal knots (1623-24). These knots are understood as nuptial by Atalide, but refer in reality to the strangulating devices of the mutes. It is this same sadism which helps Roxane stage the horrible spectacles of death as she envisages first Atalide spectator of Bajazet's death, then Bajazet spectator of Atalide's death, both grisly plays-within-plays since the joy she seeks is one of watching that spectator.

That passion, no less than the seraglio, is a prison, however self-imposed it may be. Roxane speaks of Bajazet's perfidy, but she admits that because of him she has "forgotten everything" (308); for him she has perverted her entire entourage (311–12); having committed herself she must be "repaid" or redeem herself in her own eyes and in those of Amurat: if Bajazet does not do for her as much as she has done for him, she will ruin him though she might perish as a result (320–24). It is this very statement that reveals the weakness of her position: her actions depend entirely on his (326); he may be impotent, but so is she, as long as she depends on him. This is why, when she finds out that her erotic quest is hopeless, she "breathes once more" with "utmost joy" (1273). Rid of the "cares" engendered by her passion, she can give herself over to the "tranquil fury" of her vengeance (1275–76).

Roxane is aroused before she sees Bajazet (141). Part of this is due, as I have said, to a quest for security, respectability, honor, and power; part of it is sexual. That these two parts are really inseparable is made manifest in their first encounter, when Roxane tells Bajazet that she holds his life in her hands. Her frequent allusions to this relationship — and, indirectly, to the method of death: "You only breathe as long as I love you" (510) — consecrate the immutable bond of power, love, and death. By the time she gives her ultimatum, she knows that he does not love her. We know that it does not matter: if he kills the woman he does love and marries Roxane, she will have tied him to her by his crime; her rise to respectability will be matched by his fall to ignominy; she will have risen to royal standing by enslaving a royal scion. The challenge is not meant to make Bajazet prove a love; it is uttered to turn the prince into her thing, denying his love, his origin, himself.

Roxane speaks of love and of death, and of her power to command the two. That power, like her power over people, reveals itself as just another of those "comic illusions" that contribute to Racine's vision of the futility of human effort. Roxane may say that nothing can hold her back, that she can accomplish what her love dictates (424), but what is most striking is the juxtaposition of *dessein* ("plan") and *amour* ("love"); was there ever an unsafer cause or unstabler effect? This play is the representation of a per-

Bajazet

fidious world — words such as "credulous," "perfidious," "feign," "betray," and their derivatives abound in *Bajazet* — and appearances are as deceptive as the characters. Our overview permits us to see what Roxane never realizes, that this "comedy" is being played out in a *huis clos* for her as for her intended victims. Amurat has not given power, but the illusion of power sufficient only for his subjects to betray and doom themselves. There should be no question of omnipotent or impotent ones, only of leaders and led, and all those who are led die in *Bajazet,* Roxane first of all, as Acomat's plan — not Roxane's — fails.

With such a powerful central figure, why was *Bajazet* unable to withstand the critical shift from the touching to the dramatic? Why this steady decline which makes it one of the least performed of Racine's plays today? Contemporaries of Racine pointed out that the poetry of this play was not up to the level set by previous ones. To some extent this is true; there are some clumsy lines and obvious padding, but I find the general tone to be remarkably successful. The lines do not soar, there is no elegiacal tone, but I tend to agree with Judd Hubert that in the infernal atmosphere of the seraglio such lyricism would have been completely out of place.[13] The ambiguity of desires, the stifling surroundings, the hesitations, insecurity — all that is reflected in the dense and involuted lines of *Bajazet*. Thus, when Atalide says, "Mon unique espérance est dans mon désespoir" (336: My sole hope lies in my despair), she is doing much more than indulging in precious subtilization. Her notion of self-sacrifice makes her hope that Bajazet will survive in Roxane's arms, however much such an outcome might hurt Atalide. The apparent contradiction in the line is the distillation of the turmoil within the speaker.

Where then is the problem? Is it that too few are willing to make the effort to place these problematic characters in their equivocal milieu? It is not always easy to say why a play falls from favor. In the case of *Bajazet* I can only suggest why I do not like it in spite of its many qualities. Some readers and viewers feel that the main characters have been perverted by outside forces and, reluctant liars, are not to be held responsible. I am not convinced. They lie and betray so readily that their protestations are hard to believe. Atalide, by "artifice" (353), has enjoined Bajazet to "feign" (388); he regrets his deception only because it failed (669). Roxane bemoans her credulity, the perfidy of a traitor who admits having kept a "perfidious silence" (997), but she in turn admits that she is no better (1090) and bemoans only the lack of efficacy of her intrigue (1071). As for Atalide, with a "disposition to feigning" (1573) and a remarkable lack of conscience, she seems eminently worthy of a lover whose ambitious heart is tempted by the throne (1503) offered by that overly credulous lover (742). The situations are dramatic, the roles demanding, but how can I feel any degree of interest in this devious lot? "Toucher et plaire" was the dictum of Racine. I am fascinated by the characters of *Bajazet,* but not moved; my heart has yet to find the reason which my reason perceives.

CHAPTER 9

Mithridate

IF the ability to "toucher et plaire" is any indication, then *Mithridate,* first performed in January, 1673, must be considered one of Racine's best plays. Even such Cornelian partisans as Mme de Sévigné spoke of crying as much at the thirtieth performance as at the first. A great success from the beginning, the play was the favorite of Louis XIV and his court, where it was frequently performed at state functions. With few exceptions, the Cornelian clan joined in the general praise, speaking of tears and admiration, tenderness and awe. This is not surprising, for the play bears much resemblance — however superficial — to some of the more melodramatic works of the aging Corneille.

The plot is unusually involved for Racine. For forty years Mithridate, king of Pontus, has been fighting the Romans with the backing of his younger son Xipharès while his older son Pharnace is "Roman of heart." When Mithridate's death is rumored, his two sons come to the capital to declare their love to the king's young fiancée, Monime, who is in love with Xipharès. Mithridate returns and is disturbed by the presence of his sons away from their posts. Suspecting Pharnace of having designs on Monime, Mithridate has him arrested; Pharnace, believing himself betrayed by his brother, denounces him. Though Mithridate loves Xipharès he cannot prevent his suspicious nature from gnawing at him. To discover the true sentiments of all concerned, Mithridate tells Monime that because of his age, he would rather see her marry Xipharès. Her overjoyed reaction betrays her, and he decides to marry her immediately, but she now rejects him: his treachery has released her from all vows. Before he can resolve the problem, Mithridate is called to battle, first issuing an order to send poison to Monime. She is about to take it when news is brought that Mithridate, on the verge of being taken prisoner, has stabbed himself. As he is carried off, he sees the Romans (aided by Pharnace) driven off by Xipharès. In a last act of generosity, he gives Monime to Xipharès and dies.

Racine took little more than a few names from history, forging personal links that did not exist and condensing into one day events that were spread over twenty-six years. What Racine called faithful recreation is not the dramatization of chronicles but the bringing back to life of an era and its climate. Though he had done this before, the extent of the factual deformation is unprecedented. Like Amurat, Mithridate is a cruel, devious tyrant holding the lives of others in his hand. Both *Bajazet* and *Mithridate* begin with an absence which throws a court into turmoil and gives the remaining protagonists an illusion of autonomy, but the return of Mithridate does not bring about an end to the confusion. As he describes the night battle in which he first met defeat, he speaks of utter chaos during which "we, ourselves, turned our own weapons against ourselves" (444).[1] Like that of Amurat, the court of Mithridate demands a certain reserve, even deviousness. If Xipharès and Monime are not always totally frank, it is due in large part to the respect they have for Mithridate, but no less to their fear of his jealous outbursts. To remain true to her concept of duty, to prevent her yielding to temptation, Monime orders Xipharès out of her sight. But these "noble stratagems"[2] are also comments on Mithridate's tyranny.

Though the locale is Oriental and therefore reminiscent of *Bajazet,* there are also echoes of Corneille. A plot "loaded with subject matter," the *coups de théâtre* and peripeteias that would pervade drama for the next two hundred years, the appeal of generosity — Monime reluctantly admiring Mithridate initially and eventually (1675-78) won over again by the magnanimity of the dying monarch — and dramatic uses of the "generation gap," all these are Cornelian signatures. Furthermore, the situation itself is patterned after some of the more famous ones of Corneille — a father with two sons, one faithful to a cause, the other not *(Nicomède),* or an older lover forcing a young girl to reveal a love, making the union desired by the old man impossible *(Attila).*[3] All these similarities are superficial. What is less so is that for the first and only time Racine depicted conflicts that stemmed less from inner feelings than from struggles between feelings and situations, perhaps even between the famous duty and love. For once we are faced with characters who know what they must do and barely vacillate before the task. As in Corneille, the pathos emanates primarily from the tyranny of their sense of obligation over their sentiments.

The exposition is masterful; the first lines tell all: Mithridate thought dead, the two brothers on opposite political sides and rivals for the love of Monime who had been wooed by their father, the primacy of Xipharès' love, the betrayal of the father by a wife ambitious for her child — nothing is left out but the outcome of the battle against the Romans. That first scene also displays a new poetic strength unfortunately mixed with a preciosity that can no longer be appreciated today. As I have stated, there are borrowings from Corneille, but more apparent still is a Hellenic influence, as in the touchingly noble lines of Monime ready to die, or in the relation of events whose epic style recalls that of Homer (1558-1618). Beyond these influences Racine displays a new richness of style all his own. Beyond the daring metaphors (62), the antitheses (23), and prosodic gymnastics (9-13)[4] is a denseness — often untranslatable: "C'en est fait, Madame, et j'ai vécu" (1678) — that allows a character to express his essence in a single line, as when Mithridate dies content, since his "last gaze has seen the Romans flee" (1666). Nowhere is this richness more evident than in the scene in which Monime will renounce her love forever. She will speak

> ... pour la première et la dernière fois. . . .
> Je vous le dis, Seigneur, pour ne plus vous le dire,
> Ma gloire me rappelle et m'entraîne à l'autel,
> Où je vais vous jurer un silence éternel.
> J'entends, vous gémissez; mais telle est ma misère.
> Je ne suis point à vous, je suis à votre père.
>
> (678, 696-700)[5]

Despite the poetic innovations, most of which are in the mouths of the young lovers, it is on Mithridate that we must focus our attention, for he dominates the action even when not on stage. The nineteenth-century actor Geoffroy described him best when he spoke of an ungrateful and difficult role because in it one had to join "courage with cruelty, magnanimity with dissimulation, transports of anger with the failings of love, the genius of the great enterprises with the little domestic ruses."[6] Mithridate is the greatest of men (1330) even according to Monime who does not love him. Proud — Racine, like Bossuet, Pascal, La Rochefoucauld, and all the classical writers, usually made a vice of pride; in Corneille it is a virtue, and in this Cornelian play it is ambiguous, part virtue, part vice — bold, with epic proportions, Mithridate is also devious and jealous. These two vices will lead to his downfall; purged of them, he will rise in defeat to heights he had not been able to reach in victory.

Mithridate is not the first Racinian character in whom absolute power is supposedly vested but, with the possible exception of Alexandre, he is the first incarnation of such power presented on stage with a truly exceptional character. He knows what attributes it takes to be a ruler, and he knows that he possesses them. Even in defeat he is endowed with a name and an aura that command continued admiration as he refuses to go down. Rome has backed him to the wall? He will therefore invade Rome: "Rome will never be vanquished but in Rome" (836). Geographical, political, and military realities notwithstanding, the angry passion of the king dictates a policy of grandiose madness. Racine has been criticized for displaying what some consider an ignorance of geography and politics; I would rather think of Mithridate's passionate ejaculations as dramatic necessities that Racine did well not to stifle. Mithridate is the seat of authority; as long as he lives no one thinks of questioning it. Though in love, none of the three young people dares declare himself while the king lives. When he is thought dead, they speak; when he reappears, that love must be silenced. Yet the bases for that unchallenged authority are quite varied: Pharnace, raised in Rome, simply fears his father; Xipharès loves and respects him, wanting above all to be unlike his faithless mother and remain loyal; Monime's behavior is dictated by her sense of obligation to her father's dictates. Only when Mithridate forces her to confess her love does she feel released from that obligation. Monime's heart is her own. What she feels, as long as it remains undeclared, as long as it does not regulate her conduct, is her own affair. When Mithridate violates that virtuous logic, he frees her, or rather, he forces her to obey a higher law than that of filial obedience. As she puts it, he erred in giving her back her heart (1282), or, as André Simonnet has so justly noted, he had no right to lapse into an unreliable tyranny for which Monime can have no respect and to which she owes no obedience. Having failed in this obligation to authority, he has lost its privilege; Monime can justifiably feel free.[7]

This old man who rejects pity and demands admiration (1650–52) is first and foremost a warrior; he is also a father and lover. He is far from ridiculous as his sons' rival. His précieux

Mithridate

declarations may seem comic out of context, but they are delivered with such heart — compare his attitude, however insecure it may be, with the bumbling reaction of Xipharès to Monime's declarations — that they attain acceptability. What is less acceptable is his treachery. However carefully he may excuse it, it is contemptible and betrays his fundamental insecurity. "Let us deceive whoever betrays us,... feign [and] by a clever lie reach truth" (1031-34). Ironically his lie yields another type of misinformation since the young lovers, in deference to him, had kept their feelings in check and had behaved most chastely (a behavior which he, more passionate, cannot understand).[8] When he decides to trap Monime, when he tries to find the truth by means of a lie, Mithridate is acting, but what he says is nevertheless true; to throw Monime off guard he begins with a confession: "Until now, fortune and victory concealed my gray hair under thirty diadems. That time is gone. I reigned, and I flee. My years have increased; my honors are destroyed; and my brow, shorn of its noble ornaments shows all the ravages of time" (1039-44). To be sure, the speech is prompted by stealth: blaming his old age and his many martial commitments, he wants to give her the impression that he would rather she marry Xipharès in order to find out her true sentiments. Whatever the devious reasons for the speech, its facts are only too true. The viewer's and reader's fascination must come from the doubly dual situation: on the one hand, the deception has all the chances of success because what he says is true; on the other hand, the confession itself is totally out of character: will Monime swallow the tempting bait? Keep in mind that he tells her now what she told him at their last encounter, as though he had thought it over and come to agree. This might make her fall more readily into the trap, or it might make her more wary. As Monime's confidante puts it, "does a great king descend to such deviousness?" (1148). Being righteous, Monime cannot think of Mithridate as less noble, and thus traps herself — or allows herself to be trapped. The irony here is that it is not only with a lie that he gets to the truth, but that it is by revealing himself as he is, by accentuating what he had been trying to minimize that Mithridate kills his last chance of happiness. When Monime finally rejects him, he is forced to look at himself: "Who am I? Is this Monime? And am I Mithridate?" (1383). "Recognizing" himself only when his anger dominates (1385, 1388, 1393), he shows simultaneously his grandeur and his flaw: the anger, noble perhaps in war, is "useless" against those he loves (1409).

The "crime" of the wife, the estrangement of his sons, his jealousy — all make for an emotional entanglement that reinforces the political one. The play starts with a notion of turmoil and confusion (it is in the confusion of the night that Mithridate is defeated) which at both political and personal levels will have to be cleared up before the tangles are *dénoués*. Mithridate has dared dream an impossible dream, in war as in love. We know it, and we sense in many of his more lucid lines that he knows it too. It is precisely in that lucid struggle against invincible forces that he commands our admiration. In the final analysis all the flaws that lead to Mithridate's downfall are erased by the grandeur of his exit. It takes only a moment, but what a moment!

Mithridate is both warrior and lover; he is also father. There is no need to view "you have as judge a father who loves you" (427) as ironic. The actor Baron, one of the early interpreters of the king's role, addressed the two sons — "You Pontus, you Colchos" (426) — in totally different tones of voice, so that what followed was neither maudlin nor ironic but purposefully ambiguous, with a different degree of sincerity for each son. In them we can readily see a reincarnation of the contradictory traits of the father, Pharnace embodying the selfish deviousness, Xipharès the heroism. Both sons love Monime, and here again they reflect their father's attitudes; the hesitant, almost precious Mithridate lives in Xipharès while the brutal one is to be found in Pharnace. Pharnace is doubly guilty. Xipharès is the younger and knows that he must defer to his senior (19), but that seniority, along with its privileges, entails obligations which Pharnace fails to carry out. He is not only a bad son on the personal level, but an unworthy heir in the dynastic realm.

Xipharès is Mithridate without flaws, a great warrior having his way on the battlefield yet magnanimous enough to allow Monime freedom to decide her own fate. Driven by a deep sense of loyalty which is due in large part to his desire to redeem the "crime" of his mother (363-64, 943, etc.), he consciously follows the path of generosity. A perfect gentleman, acting without coercion, he wins Monime's heart and his father's hatred by the very openness of his behavior. Xipharès is only too aware of his father's faults for which he has only scorn (49-56), but they do not alter his sense of duty and loyalty. As he tells of Monime led to Mithridate, he also tells of his mother's betrayal, of his outrage, of his efforts to redeem her shameful behavior by his valor and his allegiance. He forgets that his father is his rival (here again he shows himself a worthy son of his father: both find it remarkably easy to force love to take a back seat). Some critics have seen in Xipharès an *honnête homme* who is more French than Greek. Like Antoine Adam I prefer to see in him one of these "heroic and tender" creatures lost in a cruel world, an "ideal image of youth and beauty."[9] The young lovers, as a single entity, confront the old and devious Mithridate not only on the moral level, but on the dramatic and poetic levels as well. Never, not even in *Bérénice,* had Racine been so lyrical, so melodic. Xipharès, like Monime, is the incarnation of that poetry and, as such, is not the displaced Frenchman that some have made of him.

Monime is "the most adorable, the most exquisite, the most harmonious of the princesses of our divine Racine."[10] She is led by her heart, but a heart ruled by a great sense of right and wrong. It is this moral rectitude that makes her give up Xipharès; it is also what makes her refuse Mithridate once he has tricked her into confessing her love (1347-54). Her sense of duty is as strong as Xipharès', and she never questions her role, though her contemplated suicide could easily be seen as a search for freedom. "I had to obey. Crowned slave, I went to the marriage to which I was destined" (255-56). Given by her parents to Mithridate, she obeyed this omnipotent lord (547-50), though her first voicing of that obedience makes it quite clear even to Mithridate that she is a slave willing to submit to a yoke (551) and not a lover gladly giving her heart. From that moment on she renounces the man she loves and, indirectly, herself (1332), willingly if not gladly. The brutal Mithridate does not consider this enough (585) and compounds his error and tyranny by trying to possess the heart as well as the will. When he tricks her into admitting her love for his favorite son, he unwittingly emancipates the "slave" who is then in a position to "dare" (1277) not only to hesitate, but to bluntly reject the king who has "given back her heart" (1282). By this extraction of a confession, Mithridate has made Monime's position impossible; not only does he become unworthy — up to now she was able to console herself with the notion that she was instrumental in making happy a man such as he (1338) — but her confession will forever stand between them, lowering her in her own eyes as well as in his.

One of the great lovers of Racine, Monime is gentle yet proud, passionate yet modest. From the beginning she unveils her "only heart" (271) which feels indifference for Mithridate, hatred for Pharnace, love for Xipharès. In act II, scene vi, as Xipharès finally penetrates her reserve, she pours out her love in lines of supreme lyricism (particularly 674–710), couched in such delicate modesty that the most rigorous laws of decorum are never threatened. Yet, despite that love, she would have married Mithridate to obey a paternal order; much of her hatred for Pharnace is due to her espousal of her father's struggle against Rome (274); even her love takes second place to her sense of obligation to herself and her filial duty. This does not mean that the struggle is an easy one. She is wary of her capability to stifle her love by herself (728), and must enlist Xipharès to help her prevent any "unworthy sighs" (730): if his great heart ever felt true love, he can prove it only by forever avoiding her (707-10). When she asks him to "deserve the tears that he will cost her" (746), she is asking him to sacrifice their love on the altar of duty, to purposefully avoid her lest, weakening with each word they exchange, she succumb to the "fatal pleasure" that she simultaneously desires and fears (739–42). In a scene reminiscent of the one in which Chimène and Rodrigue of Corneille's *Cid* agree to be worthy of each other (III, iv), she asks him to make a supreme, "heroic" (723) effort against himself, so as to preserve his image and help her save hers.

At no time is Monime guilty of excessive protestations. Firm in her resolve to be true to her obligations, she adds to Racine's own Antigone a new dimension, one of *grandeur* and *honnêteté*, derived as much from Sophocles as from La Rochefoucauld. Hers is a truly great role, perfectly "classical," one which radiates pride, grace, charm, decorum, yet great tenderness. It is also a most difficult one: because of the characteristic restraint, it is entirely devoid of the stormy scenes that allow an actress to shine in roles such as those of Roxane or Phèdre; for Monime there are no ejaculations, no outbursts, gestural or vocal. Rare is the actress who can learn to live the personality and translate its tensions without appearing dull and frigid. An imaginative reader can obviously do better in that respect than all but the finest actresses — even Sarah Bernhardt and Marie Bell failed in this role — which may explain why *Mithridate* is more popular in the classroom than on stage.

Facing this tender, heroic, and highly moral young couple is the volatile Mithridate whose former glory only serves to make the eclipse more evident (1293–94).[11] While Pharnace, Xipharès, and

Monime may have ambiguous feelings regarding the past, Mithridate sees it only as one of glory and youthful power, which contrast with the decadence of the present; this is why he would like to eradicate it (1293-94). Wanting to perpetuate an illusion, he merely succeeds in giving a tragic tone to time. With each of his failures to stop the flow of events, we find a tragic vision more precisely centered on a present sandwiched between a glorious past and a far less glorious future. The ending of *Mithridate,* brought about by the titular hero's complete reversal, has frequently been declared overly optimistic and psychologically unrealistic, but neither accusation is entirely correct if this ending is viewed in light of the aforementioned interplays.

In one sense, the ending is an apotheosis of Mithridate who gives Monime to Xipharès, the reincarnation of his heroic being. In this way the couple will, as a unit, perpetuate him, his love, his every ambition, since Mithridate had earlier called Xipharès "the heir and mainstay of an empire and of a name which will be reborn in him" (1069-70). But most of all, this is an ending which, however surprising it might be, is eminently logical at the psychological level. When he realizes that he is dying, Mithridate once more becomes aware of his place in history. His anger and his love, once transmitted, are replaced at the forefront of his concerns by his nobler instincts. His "gifts" are more political than generous: he has only one son worthy of carrying on, and that son needs Monime's alliance as much as he, Mithridate, had needed it. To enshrine his *gloire,* to attain a peace far above the *trouble* and *ténèbres* that assailed him, he cements with this ultimate gift what he believes to be a victory (1666). Mithridate's last glimpse of the Romans *seems* to be one of victory, but we know that this is little more than the vanity of an empire builder at work. The war is not over, and the Romans will come back in force to destroy the vestiges of Mithridate's realm (1680-82). The play ends not in victory, but in a suspenseful anticipation. Mithridate, in death, has been allowed a last illusion. The dramatically necessary catharsis and transcendence are thus backed by psychological and dramatic verisimilitude. A fighter and a lover, Mithridate is first and foremost a self-conscious hero. Dying, he can and must give a meaning to his forty years' struggle by allowing his son to carry on. Paternal tenderness, reinforced by the admiration that one hero owes another, makes the reconciliation as logical as is the death, the only possible outcome of an impossible struggle.

The play is hardly flawless. Racine gave little thought to geographical and tactical details: the military maneuvers described by Mithridate verge on the ridiculous. Psychologically, some of the dialogues make little sense: Mithridate may thirst for communication with his sons, but how much of his military plans would this astute general divulge to a son he calls "Roman"? The major difficulty lies elsewhere, however. I have already mentioned the difficulty of Monime's role. Mithridate, vacillating between greatness and pettiness, between self-assurance and indecision (contrast, for instance, his great entrance with the insecurity emphasized by the stumbling rhythm of line 481), is treacherous for actor and director alike. It is a strong role, but how is one to set the tone for it?

The seventeenth century considered *Mithridate* a political play; modern critics, readers, and viewers see it more as a love drama with Monime as the focus of interest and Mithridate as little more than an aging spoiler. It has frequently been suggested that Mithridate is the center of two coexisting plays, one political in which he opposes the Romans, one erotic in which he opposes the young lovers. To some extent this is true, but it is obvious that Racine took great care to intertwine the two. For instance, when Mithridate sends Pharnace to Partha, he simultaneously rids himself of a rival and, by wedding him to the Parthan princess, cements an alliance needed for his fight against Rome. Our temperament may make us respond more to one aspect or the other, but Racine welded the two together.

And yet, with that change of perspective, the public allowed *Mithridate* to fall from its exalted rank. I see two major reasons for this. The first I have already mentioned: however well Racine may have welded the two dramas, the play remains ambiguous in tone, at times grandiose, at times petty, the characters caught less in a vise of destiny than in the rhetoric of their own choosing. The second reason for the decline in popularity is one that also explains its astounding success. *Mithridate* represents the age of Versailles; it represents no less the age of Quinault, pomp and sentimentality. In all of Racine's tragedies one may speak of the fate of entire nations at stake, but whereas in *Bérénice* or even *Bajazet* that fate is concentrated into a personal drama, in *Mithridate* the overwhelming historic tableau never yields to the individual plight: none of the major protagonists sees love as a prime factor — they can too easily get along without the ones they love — and for most of them, love seldom rises above gallantry or at best chivalry. Racinian psychology still drives the protagonists, but it is not as well integrated as in other plays, and the *coups de théâtre* are more reminiscent of Cornelian melodrama than Racinian tragedy.

CHAPTER 10

Iphigénie

IT took Racine eighteen months to follow up the success of *Mithridate*. He had earlier contemplated treating the subject of Iphigenia, but seems to have been torn between the two major episodes in her life: her near-sacrifice in Aulis and her role as priestess and arbiter of fate in Thauris, between Iphigenia sacrificed and Iphigenia sacrificing. He went so far as to map out a rather detailed plan of the first act of an *Iphigénie en Tauride,* which tells us much about Racine's methods of composition, but opted for a brilliant combination of Racinian and Hellenic elements dealing with the episode that released the fleet to consummate the fall of Troy. Reading his preface, one would think that Racine did little more than rejuvenate Euripides' tragedy. Not so; to satisfy the *bienséances* he could not sacrifice a maiden as virtuous as Iphigenia; for the sake of *vraisemblance* he could not, in the seventeenth century, repeat his predecessor's substitution of a hind on the sacrificial altar. Eriphile — whose name (lover of discord) is also borrowed from the Ancients — is his invention which allows him to create an entirely new play.

The Greek fleet, ready to sail for Troy, is immobilized in Aulis by a calm which, according to an oracle, will last until a maiden relative of Helen is sacrificed to Diana. He names Iphigénie, and King Agamemnon, whose daughter bears that name, is torn between patriotism and paternal love. Agamemnon yields at last to the will of the gods and of Ulysses — one of the more powerful chiefs instrumental in his election as leader of the expedition — and summons his daughter under the pretext that Achille wants to marry her before he sails. She arrives with her mother, Clytemnestre, and Eriphile, a companion who had been captured by Achille in Lesbos. Eriphile, secretly in love with Achille, hates Iphigénie and

Iphigénie

does her best to destroy her, though the latter has shown her nothing but love. When Agamemnon's real plans are discovered, Clytemnestre becomes a fury in the defense of her daughter, while Achille feels both his love and his honor attacked. Under their combined assaults, Agamemnon weakens and is ready to help Iphigénie escape when Eriphile betrays them to the oracle who, to prevent a battle between those who require the sacrifice and those intent on preventing it, reveals that the Iphigénie required is not the daughter of Agamemnon but of Helen and Theseus, a girl raised under another name until now. Eriphile recognizes herself and her defeat; she stabs herself on the alter as the winds begin to blow: the Trojan War will take place.

Once again Racine has produced a family drama, but this time all the major protagonists are of divine origin, and the gods, veritable family elders, propel the action and decide the outcome. Not *Esther,* not *Athalie,* but *Iphigénie* marks Racine's entrance into the realm of the sacred. The play, like the Greek drama it imitates, deals with gods who actively participate; they speak (in the original Calchas is merely an astrologer; here he is a priest transmitting the divine will), are spoken to, and direct the human beings, the human surrogates acting out a divine charade. These divinities are of dubious virtue. Transmitters of half-truths — how far is their oracular ambiguity from outright deception? — they are called unfair and unjust by all. In this "sacred" atmosphere there are mostly skeptics: no one doubts the existence of the gods, but everyone has serious reservations about their horrible and oppressive injustice. Blindly obeyed by the mob and an ambitious king, their cult strikes more as a superstition for the former and a tool for the latter. It is not surprising that these unattractive deities are faithfully mirrored by their human surrogates.

Eriphile has "the pride of Hermione, the selfish savagery of Roxane, the sensuality of Phèdre; and the jealousy that is all her own,"[1] all of these vivified by her love for the man whom she first saw drenched in blood as he slaughtered her people and captured her. The suddenness of her passion is still vividly in her mind: reproaches died on her lips, her anger melted; as she puts it in one of the great understatements in Racine, "I saw him ... I loved him ... I love him still" (497–502). Scheming, devious, perfidious (see act II, scene v in particular), Eriphile forever seeks opportunities to harm her rival. She accepts the charitable advances of Iphigénie only to arm herself against her and to destroy a happiness she cannot stand (506–8), for she is less intent on becoming happy than on making others miserable (766). In love with her captor, she wants only to voice her misery and make others share it, wallowing in a self-pity (1090–1126) that erodes whatever pity one might feel for her as much as does her heinous — though more readily understandable — vendetta. Iphigénie loves Achille more than life itself (1042); so does Eriphile (1104–5), but she directs all her efforts to thwart the "criminal" plot to save her rival, not to declare her own love or enhance its chances. Agamemnon speaks for his daughter as well as for himself when he says that "the most unfortunate dare cry least" (368), whereas this outsider is intent on "not crying alone or dying without vengeance" (766).[2] Though couched in irony, her death is therefore an eminently just one: having tried so hard to replace Iphigénie in the heart of Achille, she replaces her rival on an altar, though not on the matrimonial one.

This death is not the artificial and trumped up deus ex machina that some have made it to be. As I shall explain later, *Iphigénie* is a drama of identity: when Eriphile discovers her true identity, she has no choice but to kill herself. Moreover, this death is well prepared by the many allusions to the mystery surrounding her origins and to another daughter of Helen, and by the ambiguity of the oracular pronouncements. Her death is therefore neither a total surprise nor a superfluous accretion. Eriphile is "so well woven into the texture of the story that anyone reading the Euripidean tragedy after the Racinian would find the former less satisfactorily organized and unified."[3]

It goes without saying that the beloved is quite oblivious to Eriphile's problems. Single-mindedly heroic, Achille is also simpleminded. Seeing things in black and white, he fails to understand anyone, and while his posture and posturing may delay the sacrifice and thus give the impression that he has saved Iphigénie and prevented a divine injustice, a more careful reading reveals that the gods had never intended to allow things to move beyond the stage of possibilities. In the Euripidean version Achilles, Iphigenia, and Agamemnon are united at the altar; when Iphigenia agrees to die, Achilles can only concur and admire, so that only the ultimate divine intervention shatters the harmonious resignation. Not so in Racine, where the heroic Achille physically defies the gods (1734–42), though for the wrong reasons. More interested in his honor (950, 953, 957, 962, 975-92, etc.) than in Iphigénie's fate or feelings, he views Agamemnon's duplicity as a personal affront. In his most vehement diatribe against the embattled father (III, vi) it is a wounded pride, not an endangered love, that is heard. His "angered self-centeredness [is] a profound part of the gathering storm in which Racine's intended victim finds herself."[4] He and Iphigénie seldom speak the same language: selfish, he is knocked off balance by her unselfish defense of her father; offended by whatever offends Agamemnon, only her love for Achille makes her understand and forgive his outrageous outbursts; as her love makes her lucid, so does his egotism — the prime cause of his defiance of the gods (1082-84) — blind him.

Aulis is a rehearsal for Troy in more ways than one. Achille knows that the gods are bloodthirsty; he knows that his days are numbered and that his future, like his past, is written in blood; after Lesbos, Troy ... with bloody Aulis in between (1603-4). In spite of that, his fatalism is strongly tinged by indifference vis-à-vis the will of the gods: though they control his destiny, only he can determine his acts; they merely decide the outcome of the struggle, not how worthy the protagonists might be (259-64). As Agamemnon veils his face and Achille "plays the game" to establish his grandeur, we hear Racine's echo of the newly elaborated Cornelian canon which will best be voiced by Suréna, Corneille's ultimate hero, a scant four months after the première of *Iphigénie.*[5] Achille knows that he will die before Troy is taken: an oracle has announced it. To him, the veracity of that oracle is of no consequence; what matters is how he lives, not when he will die, and his febrile activity is no less a sign of his fatalism than his blasphemous remarks, futile defiance, and glorious self-assertion echoed by Eriphile who finds herself only to kill herself and thus become part and parcel of the legend Achille is writing.

Clytemnestre, the devoted mother snarling and clawing in defense of her young, is not above criticism either. As the gulf widens between her and Iphigénie, her outbursts are more engendered by her idea of what a good mother should do rather than by a pure and selfless love. No matter how angry, she always remains lucid, and her most devastating tirades, be they aimed at her husband whom she can never forgive or at her daughter's rival, show her complete grasp of the situation, her total awareness of the motives of her adversaries (656, 1289-92). Her attacks may be diverse in tone, but they are always inexorable in their search for the raw nerve that they infallibly touch. Her shrewishness does much to endow Agamemnon with a modicum of likeability.

Clytemnestre is monofaceted; chosen by all the chieftains of the expedition as their leader, Agamemnon is torn between the two roles he must play. Unable to commit himself entirely to either, he lives in fear of his righteous wife (91, 147, 394, etc.). Weak and unheroic, this political schemer looks for compromises, for easy ways out of his predicaments that are all doomed to failure. Though he occasionally shows glimpses of the greatness that must have been his when the Greeks elected him their leader (as when he stands his ground before the irate Achille in act IV, scene vi), he remains a simple human being isolated from his family (by guilt) and from his men (because he insists on avoiding the unavoidable sacrifice). Having lured his daughter to Aulis, using Achille as an excuse notwithstanding the possibility that the impetuous lover might come back in time to thwart the ruse, he must resort to new — and equally transparent — schemes to separate the victim from her protective mother. His duplicity is easily pierced by Clytemnestre who crushes him with a simple "Vous ne me parlez point, Seigneur, de la victime" (1166: You do not speak to me, my Lord, of the victim), the icy rebuke accentuated by the hammered rhythm.

When, at the end of the play, Iphigénie's "shadow" is substituted, like the hind of the legend, that bit of melodrama does not weaken the tragic intensity. Her sublime serenity and excessively submissive nature have prevented the tragic focus from being centered on her, putting the entire burden of the effort to save her life on her hapless father; he is the center of attention, of pity, of tragicness, locus of one of the most searing inner struggles in all dramatic literature. Before Agamennon can shed Trojan blood, he must pass the test of shedding his own — killing the person dearest to him. The king must kill the father in one of the most astutely presented oppositions of "le moi" and the reasons he thinks he has for living.[6] If tragicness means the utmost of suffering, Agamemnon, blamed by all, and perhaps most cruelly by his beloved daughter, is surely *the* tragic figure in this play.

What then of Iphigénie? Does she not deserve to be the titular heroine? Strange mixture of human and ethereal qualities, of royal — even divine — origin, she joyfully rushes to wed the greatest of heroes who is also of divine lineage. When she thinks herself rejected, her reactions are earthly and human. On the other hand, her love for her father goes well beyond the norms of her time or of ours; her ringing defense of him is not merely the result of its intelligibility. She has, particularly at that crucial moment (IV, iv), what Jacques Vier has called the intellectual courage to see what is right and what is not.[7] Her strength comes from this moral lucidity; so does her loneliness. Misunderstood, she is frequently unaware of the pain she inflicts, as is the case when she effusively greets her father: the verbalization of her joy at being "the daughter of such a father" (546) and her radiant glances are a torture to the man whose guilt prevents him from even looking at her (552-53). Her ebullient questions about the altar evoke only the searingly ironic and laconic "you will be there, my daughter" (578). When she later submits to his will, she defends him, but not without references to her obedience and her innocence, which deserved a different reward (1174-1220). By the same token, when she declares her love for Achille to her "friend" Eriphile, she unwittingly selects to voice her feelings the words that are bound to hurt her rival the most (618-24). Her innocence puts an additional burden on those who love her; it also separates her from them in spite of her protestations of love.

However worldly she may be in her discourses with, and feelings for, the men in her life, Iphigénie is conscious of another realm, and it is on this level that her crisis — and her transcendence — takes place. Aware of the divine and the legendary in the destiny of the men she loves, it is in their reflected glory that she wishes to bask. But in Aulis, with each revelation, each evaluation of perils, her knowledge grows, "knowledge that the values upon which she has staked her life have suffered spiritual and moral shipwreck. During those moments when her adoration of Agamemnon is put to its severest tests, and in fact reaches its utmost degree of purity, she will confront the *faiblesse* of human devotion — including the anguished inefficacity of her own progressively isolated love — and the soul-deadening demands of what has passed for such devotion on the part of others."[8] She does not yield to Agamemnon and accept death; she seeks it in spite of her love of life precisely because she must — like Achille and Agamemnon — reach beyond this moment to enter into that ordered and orderly legend in which she can best participate and fully share their glory. Early in her crisis — so beautifully interwoven with that of Agamemnon — she had seen her love — shades of Bérénice and Andromaque! — as a preservation of the past, a continuation of the past into the present, a deliberate attempt to prevent the present and the future from imposing an unpleasant reality. When the past is finally and firmly replaced, when the "new" Agamemnon has definitely replaced the old one, then she is ready and even willing to die. Achille and Agamemnon may be Homeric; Iphigénie, by subjugating all passions of this earth to a higher exigency, reflects rather the ethos of Versailles where her plight caused so many tears to be shed.

Facing this exalted young lady are a rather unsavory lot of characters: Eriphile is malicious, Ulysse cynical; Achille and Clytemnestre, by their blundering rushes, hurt the cause of Iphigénie more often than they help it; Agamemnon, unworthy father and king, deceives everyone, emitting lies and half-truths as readily as the gods he supposedly serves — and whom he eventually tries to cheat. Despite their perfidy and deviousness, the gods are nevertheless only potentially unjust: "In *Iphigénie* the *potential* injustice of the gods echoes and re-echoes only to die away in Diana's benevolent thunder."[9] In spite of the oracle, in spite of the characters, the play is immersed little by little in an aura of harmony and serenity, of order; gradually there emerges a new theology of which Iphigénie, by her long invocation (1174–1220), is revealed as the high priestess.

The gods cannot be circumscribed in a small palace or antechamber. The scene therefore is a vast camp on a beach. On one side the sea, with the fleet ready to sail; on the other woods large enough for the queen to lose her way. Even the altar is in the open, forming part of the camp and bristling with weapons.[10] The scale may be new, but Racine's predilection for enclosures persists: the queen has trouble getting in with her charge but even greater trouble getting out later, blocked like the fleet. There are many paths, but all are closed until the bloody toll is paid. In this wide open space limited only by the forest and the sea "everything, the army, the winds, Neptune" (9) is asleep and will remain so until the last.

On this sleepy beach time plays a role of utmost importance. It is a commonplace of Racine criticism to point out that, while in *Andromaque* the past weighs on the present, in *Iphigénie* it is the future that nearly strangles it: we know how the various characters will develop. Agamemnon, for instance, so worried lest he live out an unglorious old age in dull family surroundings, will, on the contrary, be covered with glory only to be murdered by an unforgiving wife. Much of the irony of the play derives from our awareness and knowledge of what the future of these people will be.[11] This omnipresent future, repository of certainty (though the protagonists have doubts about the sacrifice at hand, they are all certain about the fall of Troy), weighs upon a present shrouded in mystery.

As in *Bérénice,* time is cut into slices, the repetitions showing the unrelenting, insistent march toward the tragic moment.[12] All references to time evoke the anxiety of the poised Greeks, their frustration, their fears and expectations. Agamemnon simultaneously wants to delay time (to save Iphigénie) and hurry it (to write his chapter in history). He thus interiorizes a conflict that pits many of the protagonists against each other, and each additional degree of tension between the factions finds an analogous build-up of pressure within him. Time, in Aulis, is both torture and relief.

Here again we have a Racinian statement of human vanity as the illusory nature of the firmness of the plans of men is brought forth. Achille is ready to do anything to deserve the hand of Iphigénie though he *knows* that he will not return from Troy to claim her; Eriphile desperately seeks to penetrate the mystery of her identity though she knows that such knowledge will cause her death; Agamemnon repeats to all who will listen that he is a king of kings, yet is torn between his role and that of father and ends up playing both badly; the entire war will be fought over a woman in whom everyone has lost interest; and Iphigénie is willing to sacrifice her life to send all these heroes on their way to futility.[13]

No less illusory is the protagonists' grasp of the truth. Iphigénie "knows" that Achille has sent for her; she then, with equal certainty, "knows" herself betrayed by him, she "knows" the meaning of her father's references to the altar. Each recognition, each peripeteia is predicated on misinformation up through the final anagnorisis which is the most ironic of all. For the reader and the viewer there can be no true surprise. Anagnorisis for us is vindication, not revelation, as our suspicions are confirmed by events and oracular ambiguities are resolved as we knew they would be. Like Créon, Eriphile learns too late that to know one's future one must first accept the legacy of the past. We knew that all along. From our knowledge of the legend, from the preface, from every sense of drama, we know that Iphigénie will not die. The suspense must come from another source, and the mystery of the traditional plot is thus amalgamated to a more profound one, that of identity. Every word, every deed in this play has as sole purpose to hasten or avoid the sacrifice of Iphigénie (if nothing else, this would validate the title of the play); but which Iphigénie? And more important yet, which sacrifice? Does not this play focus on the "dynamic portrayal of a tragic enlightenment" and less on a blood sacrifice than on a "ceremony even more devastating for the intended victim: the sacrifice of cherished, impossible delusions"?[14] This recognition is not passive, "for in Racine the act of tragic recognition can become at once the most devastating and affirmative act of all, a final measure of man's grandeur and his agony."[15] Iphigénie, like Eriphile, must find herself to be herself; catharsis, in *Iphigénie,* belongs less to us than to Iphigénie.

This great tragedy is closer to the Homeric tone and aura than any other by Racine. Gently lyrical at times, it also has savage moments. For instance, the word *coeur* occurs nearly five hundred times in Racine, and *Iphigénie* has its proper share, but never before had Racine used it in such a literal, visceral way. Achille (976, 1423, 1599) and Clytemnestre (1148, 1304, 1655) repeatedly evoke the picture of a heart dripping with blood in the hands of Calchas. Nor is *sein* used metaphorically when Clytemnestre imagines the "criminal hands tearing the breast and curious eyes searching her palpitating heart for a sign from the gods" (1303-4). Uniting his firm grasp of lyricism with a new concept of the operatic, Racine created a finale of epic proportions. As a thunderclap is heard offstage and is then echoed by the sonorous line of Clytemnestre (1698), who feels it shaking the earth, Arcas, the messenger who has obviously left the altar too soon to know the true meaning of the supernatural intervention, announces that the sacrifice has been "suspended" (1704). Ulysse then enters and reveals the benevolent nature of the gods' manifestation, as his story dovetails with that of Arcas. Thus many diverse voices and instruments, representing many moments, focus a posteriori on one single time and place: the altar at the moment of the sacrifice.

Homeric, but modern. In a century that claimed to be faithful to antiquity while "civilizing" it, mellowing and tenderizing it to a tasteless pap, Racine dared show the cruelty of a bloodthirsty tribe in such a way as to move his urbane society to tears. Verisimilitude, for once, was willing to crowd convention, as an angry Achille and

Iphigénie

a no less furious Clytemnestre defied state and altar in their efforts to assert the rights of man before those of men, of the individual rather than of society. But in a play called *Iphigénie,* fate had to be served, not avoided, and so Racine invented Eriphile, a substitution at the level of the individual, not of humanity or of myth. Since the gods demanded a human sacrifice, Racine — and only Racine — dared put on the stage of his time the brutal discussion and preparation (and, however masked, the fulfillment) of such a monstrous gesture. Both Iphigénies are human, though of divine ancestry, and on the shores of Aulis in which Olympus seems rooted and which, however anachronistically, must remind the enlightened reader of those shores on which the gods immolate Hippolytus, the divine ancestors force these suffering surrogates to act out their Olympic charade. Perhaps the supreme irony is that only these two manage to transcend the moral squalor in which both men and gods wallow.

CHAPTER 11

Phèdre

IF the malevolence of the gods can be said to beat like a murderous sun on the characters of *Iphigénie,* then that sun is at its solstice in Racine's last "secular" play, *Phèdre.* "*Phèdre* distils and clarifies the idea of the perfidy of the gods nascent in *Iphigénie.*"[1] The story of Phaedra and Hippolytus is well known, but, for once, familiarity with myth and literature is not a safe guide to the better understanding of a Racinian work. Though such knowledge may help in the understanding of certain implications and relationships, it can also mislead, since Racine radically altered Euripides' and Seneca's characters. Hippolyte is no longer a misogynist, and Phèdre is neither a totally innocent victim of the gods nor an animal in rut. The play — and the original title (*Phèdre et Hippolyte*) shows this — is the subtle analysis of a complex human relationship.

Despite numerous peripetias, the plot is extremely simple. Thésée has been absent from Troezen for over six months, and his son Hippolyte is worried by that absence and by his own nascent love for Aricie, last offspring of a branch of the family exterminated by Thésée, who, wishing to see that line end with her, has forbidden her to marry. Hippolyte is also disturbed by the manifest enmity of his stepmother Phèdre. The latter is dying and, prompted by her devoted nurse Oenone, confesses that she loves Hippolyte and has tried to drive him away to keep from lapsing into adultery and incest. When the news is circulated that Thésée is dead, Oenone convinces Phèdre that she can declare her love. She does so and is rejected as the news comes that Thésée is alive and returning. Frightened, Phèdre allows Oenone to slander Hippolyte, and the nurse, afraid that he might betray her mistress, accuses him first of trying to seduce his stepmother. Phèdre is about to confess when she finds out that Hippolyte is in love with Aricie. Torn between jealousy and guilt, she again relies on Oenone. Before the silence of his wife and son, Thésée misjudges the situation and curses Hippolyte, calling upon Neptune to avenge him; the god sends a monster to stampede Hippolyte's horses, who drag the young man to his death as a remorseful Phèdre poisons herself and clears Hippolyte with her last breath.

This simple plot is housed in a remarkably balanced structure. In the first act Hippolyte confesses his love to his confidant Théramène; shortly thereafter Phèdre reveals her passion to Oenone. In the second act Hippolyte declares his love to Aricie; their tête-à-tête is interrupted by Phèdre, who attempts to seduce Hippolyte. After the return of Thésée, the confessions become silences as the two appear before the king only to refuse to speak. In the first three acts there seem to be two separate love intrigues: Phèdre-Hippolyte and Aricie-Hippolyte, with Hippolyte the focal point of both. As of act IV, however, the Aricie-Hippolyte happiness is grafted onto the Phèdre-Hippolyte impasse, worsening the queen's problem and her unhappiness: it is the prospective bliss of the lovers that makes her torment unbearable (IV, v–vi). As in *Iphigénie,* two seemingly disparate intrigues complement each other and dovetail into a single action whose literal unity is reinforced by a rich tapestry of metaphors. To better grasp that counterpoint, let us look at the characters of this play, both human and divine.

Never has a tragedy better illustrated the loneliness, the utter solitude of the tragic being, a "Promethean solitude," in which she is confined by her agony, "victim of a destiny which none of those who surround her can share, lighten, or even understand, irremediably deprived of the sole refuge which this earth offers to those pursued by the hatred of the gods: friendship, or at least human proximity."[2] Hers is a crushing role of some five hundred lines, alternatingly forceful and "spent", all of crisis, without let-up.

Of divine origin, Phèdre's impulsive libido is the cruel gift of her lustful mother Pasiphaé: "Phèdre's genealogy clearly reveals her basic conflict: she is the daughter of Minos (which means *wisdom*) and of Pasiphaé (which signifies *lust*)."[3] In her very first scene she shows — as Jocaste had done in her apostrophe to doomsday — that she is fully aware of the irrevocable bond with her past, one that she has inherited and whose weight she is just beginning to feel. That horrible legacy has been welcomed into her heart — "Plût aux Dieux..." (221-22: would that my heart were as innocent...) — in spite of her strong moral awareness. Phèdre sees everything in absolutes, including her guilt. Highly moral, she never indulges in self-deception. Like Hippolyte she suffers from a *mal,* an ailment, but unlike him she never tries to blind herself to its nefarious nature. Furthermore, whereas Hippolyte finds strength outside of it and tries to shake himself out of it, Phèdre finds élan only in her *mal:* the paradox is that her outbursts and her living-death come both from the same source. To further compound the paradox, she seeks to destroy the very quality for which she so strives: her sensual desire for Hippolyte is coupled with a yearning to possess his purity which, for most of the play, she considers intact, unconscious of the fact that by its possession she would destroy it (and unaware that she is already too late).

Such is her passion that she repeatedly thinks of Hippolyte as "monstrous" because of his immunity to her assaults. It is important here to avoid a common error: Phèdre has a certain maturity, but she is no old woman. Her children are still in the cradle; she met Hippolyte when he was already a man capable of arousing her and she was still a young bride; if she is older than he, it is not by enough to make her passion ludicrous. Phèdre is neither an old matron nor an experienced rouée; her clumsy declarations show her lack of experience; she is much closer to Aricie than to Roxane or even Bérénice. When she sees herself as young, beautiful, desirable, she must convince; her shock when she discovers that Hippolyte loves elsewhere, when she finds out that she has a rival, is a genuine surprise contradicted by nothing in the text, explicit or implied. Another common error is that of critics who debate Phèdre's guilt according to Hellenic, Roman, or Gallic laws. Phèdre is not guilty of incest because of a law or innocent because of another; she is guilty because she considers herself so. She states it quite clearly when she asks "How can the widow of Theseus love his son?" (702), and twice she speaks of her incest (1270, 1624) with revulsion; it is this disgust which takes precedence over any passion as she tries to hide her guilty secret and die in some dark corner.[4] But how does one keep a secret from an ancestor such as the Sun? How can one hope to die with such a secret when to die means to face the ancestor-judge Minos in Hades? Mythology is here not a mere source of story and characters, but a living force. The postulates of mythology make the entire universe a *huis clos* for Phèdre; more than a mere mortal by birth, Phèdre cannot hope for a simple solution to her earthly problems.

Thus Phèdre's declaration of love to Hippolyte is not a clever trap set by a rouée. It is simultaneously a sensuous statement of what could be and a dreamy evocation — "somnambulesque" is Maulnier's appropriate term — of what *could have been,* had she met Thésée-Hippolyte in the labyrinth.[5] In that dream she abolishes time, fault, and all those (Ariane, the "other" Thésée) who do not belong to that blissful imaginary world from which Hippolyte rudely recalls her with his shocked and shocking interjection (663-64), reminding her of her relationships and obligations to the real world. Awake, unmasked, the real Phèdre will then declare herself, but it is no longer a seduction that she attempts. She admits that her love is odious and calls herself a monster anxious to expiate her crime (699-704). Ironically, even this ferocious self-accusation is one of overt sexuality: her heart, which she proffers to his sword as she "feels" his arm advance to strike, leaps to meet that hand (706) as she years for this violent — and so doubly significant — love-death.

Like Phèdre, who is dying in Oenone's arms because of an illness that she conceals (146), Hippolyte is consumed by an illness he tries in vain to hide (136). Like his stepmother, he suffers because his "reason yields to the violence" of his passion (525), and like her he feels estranged from his original state, which he views almost clinically from a growing distance. There the similarity between the two characters ends.

In Euripides, Hippolytus was arrogantly proud of his chastity. Racine's Hippolyte *was* proud of it, but is now fallen, and Venus need not feel neglected by him, however reluctant his "sacrifice" may be. In his declaration of love his greatest offering to Aricie is the surrender of his "presumptuous pride" and recognition of an estrangement from his former self at which he cannot stop to marvel (524-60). Whenever he bemoans that love, it is as much to mourn the passing of his innocence — and the now clear danger of following in his father's philandering footsteps — as it is to comment on the criminality of that forbidden love. Like Phèdre he sees everything in black and white, a harsh judge of himself and of others; but in his case it is mostly because of a lack of sensitivity made even more unpalatable by a recurring momentary blindness to his failing: "Daylight is no purer than the depths of my heart" (1112) is wishful thinking at best.

This young man, the active titular hero of Euripides' play, lost that honor in later editions of Racine's play, and justly so. Though he remains of utmost importance, he is passive; he is the object of

Phèdre's and Aricie's love, the object of his father's curse, but his own reactions are minimal. Though on stage in as many scenes as Phèdre, he is eclipsed by her. Yet he is important not only to the basic plot but — and I hope to make this clearer later — to the action at both the terrestrial and the cosmic level. I refer to the disproportionate if not gratuitous intervention of the gods. Hippolyte has committed the "crime" of disregarding his father's edict. Though neither Neptune nor Thésée knows about it, he is willing to rebel against his father to obtain Aricie (1359-70). None of that explains his horrible death. Does he die, as Philip Koch maintains, to keep his purity and innocence, to keep from becoming another Thésée?[6] If such were the case, we would feel relief. I do not: in spite of Racine's prefatorial remarks to the contrary, I feel outrage.

In this beautifully balanced play, Aricie is as much a mirror for Phèdre as is Hippolyte. Aricie's happiness-in-love enhances Phèdre's unhappiness, and her purity makes the latter more conscious of her crime. Fearful and timid at times, Aricie's strong moral fiber makes her assert herself and her right to her *gloire*, in spite of her enslaved condition. She recognizes none of Thésée's rights over her (1381-84), stands up vehemently to him, and berates him for his blindness (V, iii); she refuses to follow Hippolyte into exile unless her honor is previously secured by wedlock. Like Thésée, she wishes to dominate, hoping to rule first Hippolyte, then through him Athens (572-73). In the end, having lost that tool ("objet" takes on another ironic significance in this case), she must return to a subordinate position, that of daughter of Thésée.

The pride Phèdre demonstrates at being able to dominate a heretofore untamed heart, to bring pain to it for the first time (449-450), sheds further light on her passion. Both women love Hippolyte for those virtues he had found in himself, those of Thésée — but without the latter's vices. Both women are attracted by him because he is virginal, wild, *farouche.* Both love his purity; yet both wish to destroy it in possessing him. That is the real impasse of their love, and if "impurity" and "impossible" were relative terms, one could say that Phèdre's quest is doomed even more quickly and more surely than Aricie's, because her love demands of Hippolyte a more total surrender of precisely those qualities that cannot stand compromises.[7]

Facing these characters avid of purity is one of the most superficial and self-righteous fools in tragic literature. These dubious qualities allow Thésée to reconcile his great struggles for right —

the pursuit of monsters and criminals — and his witless and remorseless amorous escapades in which he demonstrates a remarkable callousness and immunity to any feelings other than erotic self-gratification. Philanderer, his only friend is another philanderer (957-58). Irascible and unreasonable, much of his sorrow is of his own making, and, like Phèdre, he seeks to place responsibility for his failings on the shoulders of others. Totally devoid of true remorse, he sees guilt only in others. It is this aspect of Thésée that best sets off his wife's moral superiority. She may (with some justification) blame Venus and Oenone for her problems, but these attempts in no way reduce her feelings of guilt. She sees transgressions of absolute standards (which is why she cannot evoke the letter of a law for her salvation) where Thésée sees only crimes against him. This is why Théramène's *récit* fails to have the proper effect on him and why his closing tirade — frequently decried as anticlimactic — is a dramatic and psychological necessity: these final platitudes consecrate Phèdre's solitude, demonstrating once and for all that her thirst for purity was totally misunderstood. Dense, insensitive, untouched by the death of Phèdre and alien to the implications of his son's, he unwittingly rivets our attention on the dead.

Ethically he is not even the equal of "detestable" Oenone, who knows to what extent she has forsaken morality to save her mistress. With total self-abnegation Oenone has abandoned her own children and will do anything to insure Phèdre's happiness. She cannot be viewed as a mere alter ego, since she has a will and a dramatic life of her own, but there is nothing anachronistic or antitheatrical in viewing her as an overindulgent mother who lives her life vicariously through her cub and who cannot live without that outlet for her own passions. She denounces Hippolyte to defend that cub. She does not pervert concepts of ethics; she disregards them.

Descendents of gods, all these characters bear the burden of that monstrous legacy. As Thésée repeatedly — though belatedly — states, the gods accord only fatal favors (1483, 1613, 1615). Under the omnipresence of the Sun — one of the several ancestral divinities — these suffering humans play out one of the bloody acts of a long family drama. Venus had sworn vengeance on the entire race of Helios (Phèdre); Neptune had promised help to Thésée and his Diana-worshipping son. In the final holocaust, Diana is mute and Neptune helps Venus in crushing their faithful. Such is the justice of the gods.

Or is it? Is Phèdre justified in blaming Venus, who with hatred and "fatal anger" (249) pursues her and seeks her doom (257)? Only to a certain extent. We are not presented here with a fate foreign to the characters, visited gratuitously on them, as was the case in *Iphigénie*. Venus does little more than cultivate an already fertile field. Phèdre is torn between two passions (purity and sex), genetically and essentially hers. Minos and Pasiphaé as much as Venus put into her heart the fatal flame (1625) which Venus then implacably fanned. It might be said that this merely distributes the responsibility; quite so, but to more than diverse gods. Phèdre is the daughter of Minos AND Pasiphaé: both forces act within her; she gives in to the worst of these. As we shall see presently, the involvement of the other gods, particularly Neptune, is of an analogous nature.

Ambivalence and paradox imbue not only the actions of the characters and the motives of the gods; they characterize the locus itself. Troezen, the birthplace of Thésée, is a pleasant resort city associated with calm, serenity, and purification. Yet something seems rotten in this "aimable" city (2): Phèdre and Hippolyte wish to flee — the latter uses the word four times in his first five speeches — and Thésée's mysterious absence has lasted over six months. Hippolyte is heavy-eyed (134) and Phèdre is dying (144). In this normally sun-drenched place, all seek the anonymity of dark corners (155). Troezen, "aimable" Troezen, has become poisoned and profaned (1359-60). This poison, like the setting, is not localized[8] and, as in *Britannicus*, it is a leitmotif which starts as a metaphor only to become a very real and concrete factor.

Mal is the word used by both Phèdre and Hippolyte to describe their love. It is indeed a sickness, an evil in the fullest sense, whose implantation they both resisted, as they now are both ashamed of it. It leads to self-loathing, resulting from an inner alienation between the being as he or she would like to be and as he or she now is. It is a monster, foe of harmony and self-control — and in Hippolyte's case, of self-sufficiency — and recognized as such by the victims themselves.[9] That love burns in their veins like a poison. *Brûler*, a common précieux term for love, recurs in Phèdre as a hyphen between love and poison, strengthening the tie until, at the end, Phèdre's veins burn literally as well as figuratively, Medea's Athenean poison having joined that of Venus (1637-38).

I have referred to the love-monster metaphor; like the metaphor

Phèdre

of poison, it is a most complex one,[10] which begins with the Minotaur, the result of Pasiphaé's sin, a transgression compounded by Thésée's slaying of the Minotaur. It ends with the "monstrous" Phèdre's death, and with that of another monster sent by Neptune: Hippolyte, son of the monster-killer, wishing to emulate that aspect of his father, finally succeeds, though he dies in the attempt. In that dying monster's tortuous coils one can see an echo of the Minotaur's labyrinth, since its upper part is that of a bull (1517-21).[11] The Cretan labyrinth is further tied to the notion of love by Phèdre herself, as she declares her passion to Hippolyte. Why does she evoke the labyrinth if not to draw Hippolyte out of his labyrinthine defenses (743) and into the maze of her feelings where an interiorized Minotaur awaits? Though she shuns Ariane's thread and tries to reach Hippolyte in person, only Aricie manages, as Phèdre painfully admits, to find "the path to his heart" (1224).

Before Hippolyte succumbed to the *mal*, he found pleasure in taming wild horses, gifts of Neptune. As he joins the legion of those tamed by Venus (123), he neglects both Neptune and Diana in whose forests he used to hunt. Within Hippolyte we have thus the anthropomorphization of a larger struggle among the gods. It is therefore not surprising that Neptune not only sends a monster in answer to Thésée's plea, but that he personally goads Hippolyte's horses (1540). Much more than a reluctant agent, he is punishing Hippolyte's transgression.

This brings me to one of the key passages of the play for the understanding of these interconnecting metaphors, the *récit* of Théramène, a passage at times considered overlong and superfluous. It is, on the contrary, perfectly integrated by bringing into the action an important part of the plot and of the metaphorical construction, the paradox of the monster-hunter killed by the monster. It is further integrated by its echoes of earlier passages of the play. In the first scene, Théramène had spoken of the relationship between Hippolyte and his horses deteriorating because of his growing *mal*. In the final *récit* he opens by telling how the horses shared the master's lethargy. As in the first scene when Théramène had spoken of Hippolyte's loss of mastery over his steeds, so his tale ends with an even more fateful loss of control: the monster causes the horses to bolt and drag their master to his death; in both instances, a monster is involved, but now the metaphor has become reality.

One more metaphor should be mentioned, that of light and dark.

Beyond the obvious question of purity and evil[12] is one of destiny visited on men by gods. At the beginning of the play Phèdre seeks out the sun "for the last time" (172). At the end she finally dares face it. In between there is a long suspension of time which, as in *La Thébaïde,* reinforces the sense of the irrevocability of destiny. During that period both Hippolyte and Phèdre alternately seek and shun the light of day. The ambiguity is particularly striking in Phèdre's case and is reflected in Oenone's reaction to her mistress' early gesture of recoil: "You hate the light you sought" (168); the formidable nature of the ancestor has indeed broken Phèdre's resolution. Only at the end of her travails, when she has confronted the monster within, will Phèdre be able and willing to face the sun again.

These metaphors are the poetic manifestation of a complex semiology which is beyond the scope of this study. It should be noted in passing, however, that it is in large part the vehicle for the characters' intense feeling and the means by which the feeling is passed on to us. Words in *Phèdre* are seldom used to convince or to skirmish, but rather to pour out emotions. Dramatic intensity is derived not from stichomythia — which is a verbal duel demonstrating, if not efficacy, at least the hope of it — but from what is more frequently thought of as a tool of comedy, namely, parallel monologues, simultaneous litanies voiced by those who cannot communicate, sacred songs of despair whose every note we hear and make our own as it echoes in the depths of our own being in search of a responsive chord.

I have spoken of "words," and indeed they are important, but they are not everything — at least not as they are written. Phèdre's action is propelled as much by silences as by words, by what is not said as much if not more than by what is said. In the preface to *L'Amour médecin* Molière warned his readers that his comedy was written to be performed and that he advised no one to read it who could not imagine the "jeu du théâtre," the entire business that turns literature into theater. This staging — the gestures, the intonations, the atmosphere, the music, even the silences — is of the utmost importance in *Phèdre.* If Molière's admonition is ever to apply to a Racinian tragedy, it must be to this one. Such was Racine's preoccupation with this problem that he took unprecedented pains to personally coach the actress about to play the leading role.

Phèdre

Surpassing even *Bérénice* and *Iphigénie,* this is Racine's most musical, most lyrical play. The sounds and rhythms are as carefully wed to the action as the background music of a good film. There is everpresent a kind of muting in the style, a restraint in the orderly versification which, contrasting with the disorder of the passions, creates a tension that is simultaneously counterpoint and undercurrent of the psychological tension. *Phèdre,* fruit of Racine's maturity, result of his close personal relationship with the stage, is by far his most carefully orchestrated play, a ballet with words, whose success depends on the close relationship between movement and music.

Phèdre is full of movement and gestures, though these may be initiated, held back, controlled. The bodies of the protagonists must vibrate like taut strings (see 269 ff.). To these aborted gestures must be added the psychological tension. Let us for instance look at act II, scene v:[13] two statuesque groups divide our attention, Phèdre and Oenone on one side, Hippolyte on the other, giving an impression of official rigidity, of aloofness. Little by little an orchestrated crescendo is heard, from the irony of line 604 to the vertigo of 662, then, after the dramatic *tu* (670), the unleashed storm of passions until the *donne* (711), which heralds the rupture of Hippolyte's immobility. With all its power, this movement is nevertheless very delicately shaded; Phèdre begins with a gentle plea for understanding (605-8); Hippolyte's misunderstanding, his very innocence heighten her devouring passion whose expression moves Hippolyte only because he misinterprets it as referring to Thésée. The irony of the double entendres (e.g., 634) which the pure Hippolyte fathoms too late, when Phèdre's sensuality is overtly revealed (655-62), are an enriching counterpoint to this dizzying crescendo.

To fully appreciate this quality, one must also be sensitive to the delicate shading of sounds, the "voicing" of the instruments, the alternating diminuendos and crescendos that make all the more telling crashing climaxes such as "C'est Vénus toute entière à sa proie attachée" (306: All of Venus fastened to her prey). This gradation of feelings through variations of sound is seen in Phèdre's first sentences which are infused with an aura of death (153-57). Muffled sounds predominate. Her second tirade shows her reactions to her regal state and the weight of her elaborate accoutrement; the sounds enhance the idea, changing from a muffled to a keening tone: "Tout m'afflige et me nuit, et conspire à me nuire" (161: All afflicts me, harms me, and conspires to harm me); the line is evenly divided into four rhythmic sections, each one punctuated by the piercing *i* sound, a telling effect that will be heard again as Théramène tells of the arrival of "timid Aricie" on the scene of Hippolyte's death (1574). In her third tirade, conscious of her origins, Phèdre relies on relatively ringing tones (169-72) which are abandoned as she allows her love to reveal itself (176-78); the evenness of that statement then gives way as her ensuing shame is translated into rhythmic and syntactical dislocation (179-84).

Musically the best passage is perhaps the already cited *récit* of Théramène. As he speaks of the sad procession of the exiles, the sounds and rhythms recall those of a funeral march (1498-1502); the appearance of the monster is marked by an abrupt change in tonalities, with a predominance of harsh sounds which are in turn interrupted by the static description of the unperturbed Hippolyte (1527-30). The monster's rage and pain are conveyed by extremely raucous and agitated lines (1531-44), which are halted by Théramène's intervention into his own narration: his sorrow prevents further dramatization of this horrible event. Hesitating, he continues, but in a far more subjective tone, no longer a mere observer or reporter. Here again the keening tones, the open notes, prevail until the end when the neutral, expressionless tones show that he has gone beyond sorrow or despair, that he is drained of emotion.

One last example, and my personal favorite. Listen to the music of Phèdre's last — and so untranslatable! — line, the surrender of her last breath, of her last ounce of strength: "Rend au jour, [pause] qu'ils souillaient, [sliding to a sibilant pause] toute sa pureté [the last convulsive gasps as, still striving upward, she sinks in voice and body]."

I have already made mention of the importance of the eyes in Racine's theater; they are never more important than in *Phèdre,* and specifically in that magnificent confrontation (II, v), where, for the second time, Phèdre becomes simultaneously aware of the full extent of her appetites and of her frustrations. The first such awareness occurred when she first met Hippolyte: "Je le vis, je rougis, je pâlis à sa vue" (273: I saw him, I blushed, I blanched *à sa vue*). It is not for nothing that translators have been divided about that last phrase, some translating it as "at sight of him", others "when he saw me." The phrase is properly — felicitously — ambiguous, for such confrontations are *inter*views in the etymological

Phèdre

sense of the world: Phèdre reacts to her vision of Hippolyte, but no less so to the realization that he sees her. Under such circumstances the eyes are like those of Goethe's *Roman Elegies,* feeling, eager to possess, to harm, even to destroy, for only by destroying the "proud enemy" (272) can they shut out the nauseating feeling of vulnerability. These eyes besmirch the light of day (1664), and it is in such eyes that Hippolyte will see a passion of such depravity that he will be unable to look at himself without horror (718). To see through such eyes is to wish to possess; it is also to become aware of the destructive, self-defeating nature of that possessive drive which can be neither checked nor tamed. Never did Racine create a better depiction of a human being torturing and being tortured by the *regard* and, frustrated in the end, able to transcend her suffering only by "choosing the catastrophe and sinking into night."[14]

Starobinski speaks here of transcendence; that word implies activity in a realm in which Phèdre has been passive if not paralyzed until the crisis. Venus has infected her, Hippolyte has conquered her (however unwittingly), and Oenone has led her; but none of that matters, for such mundane matters, or even a struggle for life and death, are not the primary concern of *Phèdre's* action. Phèdre is ready to die at the beginning of the play, and the five acts are merely a delay of the inevitable. That is hardly suspenseful. What is at stake is her purity, her salvation in the fullest sense of the meaning, and whatever admiration we may have for her (just imagine the final tableau: the body of Phèdre still the focal point of all eyes though Thésée tries to disregard it) must surely be due to her active participation in the act of purification.

It is of paramount importance to understand the dramatic chronology of the accusation (Oenone is unleashed before the discovery of Hippolyte's love for Aricie; fear, not jealousy is the motive), and it is important to grasp the chronology of the ending: Phèdre takes the poison before she knows of Hippolyte's death, and before her own confession. She comes on stage to die, a rare break with theatrical convention in Racine, not to confess (she did not have to take poison to do that), not to lament a death she only discovers later, but to put an end to the concealment of her sin. Early in the play she wanted to die to prevent her shame from becoming public. That is the one thing that has changed in her: "She discovers in dying that something else, and better, takes place — a purification, which abolishes what she meant death to hide.... Therein especially one recognizes the very metaphor of tragedy....

Pollution and purification, illusion and self-knowledge, death and life are given an expression of their paradoxical relationship in the single image of eyes that see but do not acquire vision without suffering."[15]

As Thierry Maulnier put it, Phèdre is "the most beautiful human subject treated by Racine" because she is "the most sensual and the purest, the most attractive and the most criminal, the most complex."[16] Having reached such creative heights and won the approval of his contemporaries, what was he to do for an encore? Artistically, as well as politically, he was ready to retire.

CHAPTER 12

Esther

WHEN, in 1688, Racine yielded to the entreaties of Mme de Maintenon and broke his theatrical "silence" to once again write for the stage, he produced what may well have been the most important play of his career. Its success not only enhanced his popularity and that of his secular plays but it allowed him to solidify his position at a rapidly changing court. *Esther* benefited Racine more than any other single play. That is not its only claim to importance, but it certainly is not its least. The personal property of the Saint-Cyr School, *Esther's* success was one of esteem rather than of numbers. Racine, ever the professional, had spared nothing to make a success of this "girls' exercise." The beautiful music by Moreau was perfectly wedded to the lyricism of Racine's lines, the combination allowing the innocent young ladies to create a most touching spectacle. Yet much of the success of *Esther* must be ascribed to the fact that one could see it only by royal invitation; it was a mark of favor to be invited, and praising it was the minimum repayment. Mme de Sévigné, writing to her daughter (February 22, 1689), could not sufficiently praise the perfect union of music and poetry, the "sublime and touching" interpretation of Holy Writ, but she was most pleased at being able to exchange a few platitudes about the play with the king himself. In short, the "girls' exercise," as Racine calls it, had become a court exercise, with *Esther* a play-within-a-play and the outer spectacle staged and directed by the Sun-King in person.

There is no doubt that the first performances of *Esther* by the young orphans of Saint-Cyr were a most moving spectacle. Yet the play is seldom performed for several reasons. As he states in his preface, Racine had for a long time dreamed of "tying, as the ancient Greeks had done, the chorus and song with the action, and to use for the praise of the true God that part of the chorus which the pagans used to sing the praises of their false divinities." Though *Esther* is called a tragedy, though the choruses and musical intermezzi were published separately that year, there is no doubt that Racine thought of a single well-integrated unit. The time Racine spent personally coaching the girls, his close collaboration with the composer Moreau attest to his intention. The rumors that flew during the months of composition spoke of "opera" as often as "tragedy," and all gave Racine credit for working hard on the integration. He was writing a libretto, deciding what would be sung and what would be recited, with the music contributing much to the total effect. In his own preface Racine gave full credit to Moreau for having written the most appropriate music possible to enhance the meaning of the lines and the thrust of the action. Racine rehearsed the girls in their diction; Nivers, the royal organist, rehearsed the singing; and Moreau prepared a full professional orchestra to second the singers (augmented by the singers from the king's chamber). All in all, thirty-five to forty instruments and as many voices were added to the dramatic interpreters.

In spite of this the music has always been relegated to a secondary level, either dropped entirely or replaced by the work of whatever composer was popular at the time. Without the music the play is doomed. The choruses are not only vehicles for edification, they are an intrinsic part of the sacred aura and intense lyricism without which *Esther* becomes a second-rate morality play. The tragedy is quite brief (1286 lines); the choruses take up approximately one-third of the lines, but with music and repetitions they are much more important than that mere number of lines would indicate. With the music they establish a mood, an aura; while definitely part of the action they cannot be expected to contribute to either plot or character development. Eviscerate them, and what is left of the play?[1]

Overcompensation for this neglect has also frequently harmed the play, as when performers are selected for their singing voices rather than their acting ability.[2] Furthermore, the play demands an a priori acceptance of a certain naive simplicity. The religious involvement that was part of the life at Saint-Cyr is very difficult for a professional troupe to duplicate, and even where it succeeds in part, what may have been touching in the mouth of a school girl inevitably becomes mawkish or silly when presented away from a milieu such as that of the premiere. All this must be kept in mind. As Molière once said about one of his comedies, this play was written only to be performed, and I advise no one to read it unless he can discover in the reading all the *jeu du théâtre,* that is, the music, the gestures, the very aura that must have pervaded its first performance.

The plot is taken from the *Book of Esther.* The Jews, captives of Assuérus, are hated by the latter's minister Aman, who obtains a royal decree for their extermination. Esther, the king's new bride, is a Jewess, though only her coreligionists know it; urged by her uncle Mardochée she throws herself at the mercy of the king, pointing out that his minister has slandered the Jews who constantly pray for him and whose loyalty is proven by the fact that Mardochée once warned the king of a plot against him. Assuérus, won over by Esther's pleas, punishes Aman, honors Mardochée, frees the Jews, and allows them to rebuild their temple.

Voltaire thought that Racine's plot was preposterous, lacking in realism and verisimilitude. While that may be true, how could Racine have done otherwise? No major change to such a sacred text would have been condoned. What few changes there are were made to soften aspects of biblical savagery. In the *Book of Esther* Xerxes orders a massacre of the Jews. Feeling then that the order cannot be revoked, he issues a second one, that they be warned and allowed to defend themselves, which they do, slaughtering 75,000 men, women, and children. In *Esther* the first order is rescinded and the Jews are declared equal and thus free to kill their would-be assailants. There are other minor changes, such as Assuérus' dream, but most of these have a purely metaphoric value or were made for the sake of decency, particularly in view of the young actresses. For instance, in the original Esther is selected — like Roxane — because of her amatory ability; in Racine her victory at first sight is due undoubtedly to a divine intervention.

The fidelity to Holy Writ is not limited to the plot. With strong verbal echoes of the *Psalms* and *Jeremiah,* the very spirit of the play is biblical. Some critics have stated that Racine had taken a story out of the *Old Testament* and given it a *New Testament* flavor, but as Jean Pommier has said, there is no easy dichotomy between the former's God of vengeance and the latter's God of love. Such a God of love, of benevolence, one whose yoke is beneficial, is very much a part of the *Old Testament,* and it is that part that the *New*

Testament chose to stress, diminishing the other. In short, Racine put nothing into *Esther* that is not already in the spirit of the original.[3]

This raises another question of transposition. *Esther* is frequently thought of as primarily a *pièce à clef,* the "key" allowing us to see historic characters and events of Racine's time presented under a thin and rather transparent veil of fiction. This must be taken with a grain of salt. Esther's piety does credit to Mme de Maintenon, whose desire for a pious solitude away from court is shared by the biblical queen; the deposed Vashti may remind one of Mme de Maintenon's predecessor, Mme de Montespan; but the rest of the frequently presented analogies are harder to defend. Louvois, the powerful minister, was rapidly falling from favor, but he was not yet out and no one would have dared paint him as Aman. The angers of Assuérus are truly oriental and conform to the biblical portrait, but would an astute court politician such as Racine so depict Louix XIV? Are the persecuted Jews to be likened to any broadly or narrowly defined sect? Do they not more probably reflect Racine's distaste for any kind of persecution, be it of Protestants, Jansenists, or a specific order? In the pleas for the protection of the king and the realm, especially in the prologue[4] and the choruses, it is easy to see a reflection of the general fear of France confronted by the coalition of her foes. By the same token, if a "key" must be found, if parallels with the century of Louis XIV must be established, why look beyond the broad, general one to which Racine pointed in his preface? The choice of the story of Esther was obvious because it, like the life of Mme de Maintenon, was a perfect example of a growing trend, one of "détachement du monde [worldly things] au milieu du monde même [in the very heart of society]." Love of God without misanthropy, that was the new rule at Versailles; that is the subject of *Esther.*

This then is a biblical tale which Racine could easily have turned into another oriental orgy of lust and blood, but he wisely — from the political point of view at least — chose to make of it an edifying tale of devotion and piety. The characters are instruments of God, and justly so, in view of the circumstances of the first production. We do not see, as in so many of Racine's secular dramas, the vanity of human endeavor, but the positive side of that coin, the certainty of divine guidance, not merely the misery of man abandoned by God, but the grandeur of man with God.

I have said that *Mithridate* is living history rather than dialogued chronicle; *Esther* is dialogued morality. There is a psychological and moral polarity predicated exclusively on alliance with, or estrangement from, God. Mardochée is closest to God, Aman furthest removed, with Esther and Assuérus spaced out between the two poles. Accordingly, Mardochée is omniscient; Esther readily understands her role if not the details of the motives; Assuérus, creature of moods and passions, eventually sees enough light to serve the cause (without the *honnêteté* of a character such as Corneille's Polyeucte, he is nevertheless a virtuous pagan, his choleric character and blind gropings obviously the result of his temporary estrangement from God); but Aman never understands what is going on, either on the political level on which he is outwitted or on the spiritual level whose very existence he ignores.

The Jews are a people in exile, yet consider themselves chosen. Esther has surrounded herself with pure young "daughters of Zion," and both she and Mardochée refer to all non-Jews as "profane." This theological dichotomy is resolved at the very end of the play when an enlightened Assuérus appoints Mardochée as his prime minister. From the beginning Mardochée is endowed with the foresight of a prophet, aware of God's methods and knowing who is chosen to further them (213-14). While his dramatic importance is slight, it is he who shows the way to a floundering Esther and who will eventually guide a monarch obviously endowed with divine attributes.

Esther is the key instrument of God and as such is protected by Him (72-73). "Her conquest of the conqueror is shown, not as the triumph of passion, but as the victory of the weak over the powerful, the triumph of docility over ferocity that symbolizes the conquest of the temporal by the divine.... So in *Esther,* the love conceit ... expresses the triumph of divine love. Esther the concubine is only the docile instrument by which God transforms the ferocious oriental despot, so that 'like a docile river,' he 'obeys the hand that changes its course.'"[5] Privately Esther abhors the pomp to which she must submit as queen and seeks only communion with God. She is "weary of vain honors, and seeking [her]self" (108), yet full of will and craft when it comes to saving her people, for which she receives the aid of God. Certainly less sensuous than the Bible's Esther, she is nevertheless quite clever in her relationship with the awesome Assuérus and anything but naive in her forceful pleas to God; though she is never dishonest or scheming, she is not simpleminded either.

From the start, then, hers is an ambiguous situation, openly a triumph, since she has been chosen queen and has been reunited with her dearest friend, but privately a bitter one, since she so totally identifies with her people in captivity. These two voices intertwine throughout the first act, rising in a crescendo as the danger to the Jews becomes more pressing. It is then that, over these two voices, a third one is heard, that of God. It is He who had told Elise, through a prophet, that Esther was safe and laden with honors; it is also He who sent with her the message that "the God of Hosts will make His mighty arm manifest" (20-21). It is His voice now, coming out of the mouths of the girls in the chorus, that permeates the closing of the first act and sets the tone for the rest of the play. Whatever struggle goes on at the terrestrial level, its outcome has already been decided. Zion is saved; only the extent of specific suffering, of individual plights, remains to be decided. This God, like the pagan divinities of Racine's secular tragedies, will have His way; whatever suspense the play can afford must reside in the human pawns' suffering, not in the outcome. Mardochée's entrance (I, iii) and announcement of the peril of the Jews merely defines the immediate danger; his orders will situate Esther in the struggle, but the voice from on high is in no way stilled or muffled by this. That voice points to a solution beyond terrestrial strife and anguish. Evil men may propose, but God will dispose; Zion, once great, is prostrate, but it *will* rise again. That third voice — the chorus so closely tied dramatically and symbolically to Esther — may not advance the plot, but it is part of the tragic action.

However strong that voice might be, it cannot with verisimilitude pit Esther directly against the Jews' archfoe, Aman. Such a battle, for all its spiritual importance, must be fought on a secular level, and this is where Assuérus must enter the fray. Moody, choleric, somber, Assuérus is a "proud lion" who does not know God (288) but who, for all his formidable physiognomy, wishes to do the right thing. In the blind floundering of his "profane" world he is at the mercy of evil counselors and of events, subject in turn to melancholy and choler. He is above all a lover, and it is through his love for Esther that he is lifted out of darkness into light and peace of mind — though he never truly achieves political astuteness. Gullible believer in Aman's deceptive facade, it is ironic that he condemns him on false evidence; when he surprises him begging for mercy at Esther's feet, he thinks that the fallen favorite is daring to lay a hand on his queen (1168) and sends him to his death.

The metaphor of light and dark, so important in *Phèdre,* is also present here. Assuérus flounders in darkness and nightmare until his eyes are opened by Mardochée, who is then invited to "shine at his side" (1179). Esther, Hydaspe, and the king himself all speak of somber silence and black chagrin characteristic of Assuérus (71, 674, etc.). God, on the other hand, is surrounded by light, and the eternal light of peace (803, 807, 810) is only for the just. Only after Assuérus finds that path to light is he rid of his black moods.

Just as Zion must think of its glorious past in its hour of destitution, so must Assuérus refer to his annals as proof of his omnipotence while in the throes of a nightmare (one of Racine's few "inventions" in this play). It is in their past that both the Jews and Assuérus find solace, reassurance, and an indication of what must be done to save the future.[6] Assuérus may not know it but he, like Esther and her uncle, is an instrument of God. When Esther dares enter the throneroom without being summoned, she faces death; seeing the king's anger, she faints; when she awakens her first words are "What salutary voice orders me to live and calls back my fugitive soul into my breast?" (641-42). On one level it is easy to say that her revival is the result of Assuérus' "live" (639), but her next tirade (645-53) which ends with a direct quotation from the *Psalms,* links his secular throne to a higher, more formidable one, a parallel that had already been suggested by the reference to Israel as the bride of God (257) as Esther is the bride of Assuérus.

God is both father and husband to His people (257); so is Assuérus. Aman, on the other hand, sees only the power, not its obligations. While Assuérus, like the God of the covenant, puts value on his word and insists on rewarding virtue (553-54), Aman has no sense of justice, duty, or proportion (II, iii). More than any other character of Racine, Aman is guilty of unmitigated pride. It is from his offended pride that all his other vices and misdeeds originate. Though he is fairly lucid as to his methods of operation (483-514) and speaks with utter cynicism of a new order from which honor and rectitude will be banished, this judgment, wholly derived from his overinflated concept of self, can only lead him to disaster.

Twisted by his megalomania, his words lose all meaning. He speaks of a "just anger" aroused by Mardochée's "crime" of "insolence" (470-77). Seeing himself as a quasi-divinity who has created himself and his king (866), he believes that the Persians are right to have a "holy" fear of him and that it is the Jews who are profane by lacking this fear. His own lies and slander appear to him quite proper while Mardochée's "treasonable" attitude (511) demands "justice." Even his wife warns him of his blindness — she sees that he wishes to immolate the Jews only to his pride — and of the impending doom which his obdurate immorality beckons. As Judd Hubert points out,[7] Aman's vanity is of such proportions that it stifles all intelligence. Thus when Assuérus asks Aman how to reward a loyal subject (the king thinks of Mardochée, but Aman thinks the reference can only be to himself), Aman exuberantly speaks of "merit to be honored and faith to be crowned" (612), but dwells exclusively on the exterior trappings of power and gets so involved in this rhetoric that he forgets that the man who would lead the horse of the honored subject could be none other than himself, the man second only to the king. Mardochée has refused to honor the trappings of power that Aman pompously parades at the gates. Aman's overreaction leads to the comic situation of his having to lead Mardochée's horse in a no less empty and senseless parade of pomp, the irony of divine justice being a masterfully presented antithesis of Aman's own concept of values.

Early in the play Assuérus gropes in the dark, lashing out randomly and repeatedly asking for enlightenment (577, 708, etc.). By the end of the play he has transcended that level, joined by Esther to Mardochée in a glorious triumvirate ready to do God's work on Earth. Though "profane" he can then bask in the reflection of the "original splendor" forecast for a reborn Zion. Aman, never aware of the true nature of the struggle, is not only killed but, since his vileness is the very antithesis of the realm that is being created, is followed in death by his entire progeny. The sterility of his policy — in contrast with the metaphors of fertility and nature associated with the Jews — thus leads to the destruction of his seed.

Esther contains many standard Racinian ploys, but it does not deal with a simple palace intrigue. There is no *huis clos,* for this drama takes place in God's realm, in which the standard notions of time and place are meaningless. The biblical aura is enhanced by the disjointing of time and place. *Esther* does not have a smooth-flowing plot, but a static action with three settings reminiscent of a medieval triptych, the three tableaus being Esther facing Mardochée who instructs her in her duty; Esther, unsummoned, facing

Assuérus; and Esther confounding Aman in the presence of Assuérus. The theatrical and religious experiences are obviously inseparable, linked by the sublime poetry.[8] *Esther* may be just a "school girls' exercise," but it marks the transition to a totally different sphere of inspiration. When Racine saw the dramatic potential of that and incorporated it into the system that had allowed him to write *Phèdre,* he created *Athalie,* one of the great plays of all time.

CHAPTER 13

Athalie

URGED by the King, Racine agreed — perhaps reluctantly — to write a second play for the young ladies of Saint-Cyr. Produced in 1691 *Athalie,* like *Esther,* is a biblical play with overtly didactic goals; the plays are nevertheless radically different. *Athalie* is a play of reconciliation: reconciliation with Racine's Jansenist mentors of yore, reconciliation with a relatively kindly divinity, reconciliation most of all with many of Racine's previously elaborated ideas on theater which had been abandoned for *Esther* — though even in this last play, for reasons I shall touch upon presently, the poet did not return to a psychological drama that is propelled by the passions of complex characters.

The story of Athaliah is found in 2 *Kings* 11 and in 2 *Chronicles* 22–23. Joram, king of Judah, has married Athaliah, daughter of Ahab and Jezebel, rulers of Israël. Joram dies and his son Ahaziah succeeds him, only to be killed by Jehu, appointed by God to exterminate all the followers of Baal. To avenge her son's death Athaliah attempts to wipe out the race of David by slaying all her grandchildren. However, Johosheba, sister of Ahaziah and wife of Jehoiada the high priest, rescues one child, Joash, concealing him in the temple. After some years, learning that Athaliah wishes to destroy the temple, Jehoiada brings matters to a head; enlisting the aid of the Levites, he declares Joash king. Athaliah, hearing the people's acclaim, comes to see what is going on and is killed.

Once again Racine managed to make something of nothing. True, the Bible had supplied him with a story, but he used the quasi-totality of that story as an a priori, concentrating our attention on a crisis which is entirely spiritual, whereas in the Bible its few lines are entirely taken up by tactical matters. The play opens with one of Racine's greatest expository scenes which gives not only the entire a priori, location and time, but situates the characters in the liverse camps and sets the solemn tone. Abner, an officer of Athalie who has remained faithful to God, warns the high priest Joad that the queen plans to destroy the temple. Joad reassures him and decides to precipitate matters by declaring Joas king. Athalie, who has had a dream in which she is killed by a gentle-looking boy in priestly vestments, comes to the temple where she recognizes Joas as the boy of her dream. She questions him and is so touched by the wisdom of the boy's answers that she asks him to follow her; when he refuses, she leaves with dire threats. Mathan, priest of Baal, has come to demand Joas, knowing that his request will be rejected and intent on using this as a pretext for the murder of Joad and the destruction of the temple. Joad curses Mathan and arms the Levites. Joas is told of his identity and proclaimed king, as Athalie and her army surround the temple. Athalie makes one last attempt at reconciliation: she demands Joas and the treasure of David alluded to by Joad. The latter pretends to agree and asks that she come into the temple to obtain what she wants. She enters and is surrounded by the armed Levites as we are informed that her army, hearing of Joas' crowning, has dispersed and that Mathan has been killed. Athalie is dragged out of the temple and killed in turn.

As can be seen, this is a simple plot. The forces that confront each other have been set for some time, with tensions building up. Once the dream sets matters in motion, there is no need for complications, and Racine does not add any, contenting himself with creating tensions by juxtaposing decisive and vacillating characters so that the message of the play comes forth loud and clear for, like *Esther, Athalie* was intended as a didactic exercise. Its basic plot is that of a rebellion, but that is merely a vehicle for a message. If there is any suspense in this drama, it surrounds the question of whether or not God keeps His promises or rather, of whether God, having kept many minor promises, will keep this most important one concerning the preservation of the house of David by means of which He would eventually tear the Jews from their temporal, secular world to allow them to enter His eternal one. Historically, the importance of this story is that it deals with the preservation of the "last hope of the hapless Jews" (1651), but that is only part of the key. Metaphorically and prophetically, Joas is more than a king-to-be. Racine, by his frequent references to God's promises, by linking the importance of Shavuoth to that of Pentecost, uses Joas and his story as a hinge between the Old and the New Testaments. Joas, being the last of David's lineage through which God was to bring redemption, is the only possible prefiguration of Christ.[1] "Can even Heaven bring life to this tree that has dried down to its roots?" (139-40) is the only question that matters, and the answer will come in the form of a divine intervention to save Joas.

Never had Racine so carefully selected a time and a place to suit the action. The temple, built on the site of Abraham's sacrifice, is a holy place of awesome past and no less awesome future. Only in such a locale can justice prevail, for it is a place of God without Whom there can be no righteousness according to the severe Jansenist canon. "By crossing the threshold the queen leaves her temporal realm to enter into that of God, from which there can be no return for her, be it spatially or spiritually. The hermetic separation between the secular empire of Athalie and the sacred Temple reflects the absolute difference between damnation and salvation."[2] As Joad discovers in his prophetic trance, the "pure gold" of Joas will be turned into "base lead" (1142) once Joas leaves the temple. To fulfill Athalie's final curse — "I hope that indocile to [Joad's] yoke, tired of [his] law, faithful to the blood of Ahab which he received from me, true to his ancestor, like his father, one will see the detestable heir of David abolish your honors, profane your altar and thus avenge Athalie, Ahab and Jezebel" (1784-90) — once out of the temple, Joas will no longer be able to effectively combat the evil within him; he will stoop to crimes, including the murder of Joad's son, Zacharie. As Pascal put it, and as all Jansenists repeatedly affirmed, "grandeur of man with God, misery of man without God" — that is the story of Joas.

This action takes place on the most symbolic of feasts, Shavuoth, Pentecost. By tradition, this is when God gave the Law on Mount Sinai; in the Pentateuch it is called *hag hakatzir,* the Feast of the Harvest. To this day both these elements permeate the service in synagogues decorated with flowers and fruit where the *Akdamut,* glorifying God and Torah, is read. To recall the giving of the Law many synagogues hold confirmation ceremonies on that day. For Christians Pentecost is all that, but more as well; it celebrates the descent of the Holy Spirit upon the Apostles gathered for the Shavuoth festivities. To commemorate Peter's first sermon followed by mass conversion and baptism, many Christian churches still defer baptism until the vigil of Pentecost. The manifold significance of the day is obvious, and the play has a message that is no less so; the literal lessons of the Old Testament are echoed by the more metaphorical ones of the New Testament. The salvation in the temple heralds another one, more distant, yet even more important.

Such an aura is, of course, closely linked to the notion of time. *Eternel* is a key word, used very frequently, though it can have real meaning only for God. For the others, even Joad, who has such a firm grasp of the future and its importance (since he is willing to sacrifice himself, his family, his people's present for that future), there is only a past, a present, and a future; eternity, being atemporal, has no place in that tripartite chronology.[3] Dramatically, eternity has no meaning, and so Racine insisted on maintaining our attention focused on the dramatic present, by giving us an uninterrupted "theatrical adventure." The history of *Athalie*'s successes and failures is the history of the struggle between those who respected Racine's intention and those who would compromise and adapt.[4] *Athalie* was created as a total spectacle, with intricate machines, great music, and a large chorus. This grandiose conception is not gratuitous. Like the vocabulary, the décor has evocatory power. So do the machines: when the curtain is pulled aside in the last act, it reveals Joas to Athalie; when the back wall swings aside, it is not to let the outside in, but to reveal a part of the temple even closer to the holy of holies. By the same token, the role of the chorus is to maintain the aura of sacredness that pervades the scene. There are no intermissions, no breaks between the "acts" linked by the choral interventions which are entirely natural. Its songs of praise, of lamentation, of fervent hope and despair, all these are natural, relevant, logical echoes of the spoken word whose themes, repeated and enhanced, are thus raised to the level of leitmotif. They are an intrinsic part of the action in form and content. Linking the acts which thus flow without interruption, the chorus insures the maintenance of *all* the unities.

The didacticism of the chorus whose lines are full of pious maxims (as are all the lines dealing with or uttered by Joas) has at times been dismissed by readers as puerile. This shows the dangers of reading without awareness of the *jeu du théâtre*. The poetic diversity of the chorus' lines is an indication of the importance of the form.[5] Those who belittle them do not see beyond the surface of the meaning. To read *Athalie,* one must hear the music, and not so much Moreau's beautiful melodies — though they are extremely important — as the music of Racine's own lines. The examples I might cite are numerous: the brutal evocative power of Athalie's dream cannot be realized without the sounds of the words; the changes of tone and rhythm translate to perfection the superficial pride crumbling as the parallels between mother and daughter are revealed to Athalie herself (464-543). There can be no better example of the unity of the words and music — and of the importance of the musicality of the words themselves — than the prophecy of Joad (III, vii). As the chorus, with full orchestral accompaniment, asks for the voice of the Lord to be heard, Joad invokes the Heavens. The full orchestra introduces the first line of his vision: "Comment en un plomb vil l'or pur s'est-il changé?" (1142: How has the pure gold changed into base lead?), a slow tempo, echo of Jeremiah's *Lamentations* (IV, 1) whence Racine has taken the central image of adulterated gold; the sorrow grows in intensity, and Joad's lines have a music all their own that rises to the pathos of the women and children driven into exile, and reaches a crescendo with the apostrophe "Temple, renverse-toi; cèdres, jetez des flammes," followed by the decasyllabic "Jérusalem, objet de ma douleur" (1152-53: Temple, crumble; cedars, burn ... Jerusalem, object of my sorrow). When the chorus and "symphony" call on God to remember His generosity to Zion, Joad interrupts with his vision of the Redemption, exulting in lines of jubilation (1159-74) whose varied meter marvelously sets off the key passages of the eventual triumph of God. In these lines certain repetitions may be primarily rhetorical, but, as Jean Dubu has keenly observed, they have a no less important musical value: "Pleure, Jérusalem, pleure" (1144), and "Lève, Jérusalem, lève ta tête altière" (1166) have assonantal and alliterative values that greatly enhance the letter of the message.[6]

The music is much of the message. Beyond the dead and intellectually revived faith of the Greek, Racine rediscovers the Aeschylean concepts of tragicness in a living faith which contains the seeds of a stark fatality. This is a tragedy, "perfectly unique, perfectly solemn," which calls not only "for pity of man for man crushed by destiny, but also for the exaltation of the very power that crushes him,"[7] and to fully capture that feeling only a poetry evoking "the voice of the living God" (1497), "the voice of the Almighty" (1748), is appropriate. It is this stirring music that makes *Athalie* the masterpiece that it is.

To maintain this aura of holiness Racine must have the help of an audience which, like Joad during his vision, can see beyond the temporal. Joad sees three misfortunes, each one worse than the preceding one: the personal tragedy of Joad's son murdered by one he also considers his son; the national tragedy of an enslaved people; the spiritual ruin confirmed by the destruction of the temple. Beyond that picture of decadence arises one of rebirth, of a new Jerusalem to which a multitude will flock for a universal redemption. This is, of course, the reinforcement of an already existing pattern; the separation of secular and religious power is seen as leading to the disintegration of morals and of the society thus bereft. Athalie's palace faces the temple; Mathan is Joad's peer; only Joas, by reuniting temporal and ecclesiastical power, could rule with the grace of God. This, as we can see through Joad's eyes, is not yet to be; the end of the play is far from being the end of the story: the future is even more important than the present and, for that future, the present must be sacrificed.[8]

All this is to be seen as a validation of Joad's sacrifice, of his method, the end justifying the means. That is the formidable a priori of faith, the mental and emotional leap that the action demands and that the characters make so difficult. Racine has invented some characters (Abner, the vacillating general of Athalie; Salomith, daughter of Joad and leader of the chorus), and he has fleshed out those he drew from the Bible, but most remain rather monofaceted. Is this due, as some have suggested, to the fact that the play was meant for young girls to understand and present? Is it not rather than the biblical origin of the story and the morality involved demand such a single orientation for the main actors in this drama of salvation? Whatever the reason, the result is that these creations of Racine — with the exception of a few secondary ones — are rather unsavory.

Zacharie, as pious as Joas, has learned the lessons of his father well. His main interest to me is the genuine love he bears Joas; in view of what we know about the future, his virtues add an ironic twist to Joas' upcoming career. Josabeth's role is also minor; the more's the pity. Totally devoted to her family, devout, proud of her husband whose faith in God she shares, she is the only character endowed with a truly human dimension. Unable to share Joad's optimism, she evokes fear and pity through her nearly palpable emotions. When these are calmed, the play rises entirely above the human level. Abner, torn between his temporal allegiance to Athalie and his spiritual one to God, is more complex than most, though his role is very minor. Full of fears, uncertain about the future, he is nevertheless unshaken and unshakable in his belief in God. He may not be optimistic insofar as this God's intervention in his favor is concerned, but he does believe in Him. He is no less torn in his view of Athalie: though he respects her, he despises her beliefs. Aware of his own worth, he is quite capable of stating his mind to her and, in so doing, of using some reproachful irony (450).

Athalie, whose role is quite brief but whose presence is all-pervasive, is a relatively enlightened tyrant who has had a certain success in bringing peace and contentment to her realm. Pragmatic, she is ever intent on seeing and examining things with her own eyes; she judges people, even God, by the visible effect of their will, not by words (733). Whatever her suspicions might be, she is never satisfied until she has seen with her own eyes: "I am satisfied: I wanted to see, I saw" (736–37). Unfortunately for her, her vision is a literal one; she is moved by evidence, not faith, and that evidence, limited by the lack of faith, is incomplete and deceptive. As the play develops, the protagonists become aware of a change in her. Whereas she was known to be hard, unyielding, quick-witted, and clearheaded, she grows moody, uncertain of herself and of events. She who used to know the meaning and value of time now wavers and wastes it while Joad becomes decisive. Basically unrepentent, endowed simultaneously with an awesome madness and an ironic lucidity — witness her last lines — she is unable to partake of the peace that she has assured her kingdom, "Cette paix que je cherche et qui me fuit toujours" (438: that peace which I seek and which ever eludes me), she best characterizes the Pascalian notion of the misery of man abandoned by God.

The corruption of her heart is echoed by her priest Mathan, a former Levite, apostate without the benefit of any faith, old or new. Caricature of a casuist, he can reconcile any behavior to any faith, a self-gratifying cynic who uses religion and superstition for his own advancement, an ironic foil for the queen's many fears. His apostasy was due to hurt pride, and all his vindictive efforts are now bent on the destruction of the temple and of Joad. Such is the violence of his hatred — even his confidant is surprised by its virulence — that his normal lucidity is hampered by it, preventing him, for instance, from understanding the meaning of Athalie's hesitations. Warped by his jealous pride, he cannot believe in any god, in his officiating, or in himself, and is totally dishonest, even with himself. There is no doubt that Racine had little use or respect for the priest-courtier of his time; Mathan the sycophant is one such: he has become priest of Baal because he has properly courted Athalie; like the worms he sees making their way through the idols, he is a sign of the corruption and vanity of the temporal as represented by his queen.

Yet this great manipulator of men cannot understand what is going on in this particular struggle in which all his many real qualities are for naught, and he senses it. Something gnaws at him, a vestige of that "superstition" he mocks in others. However proud of his apostasy he may be, he cannot rid himself of a fundamental fear of God, and it is this vestige of his past that angers him most. His ultimate desire is to rid himself of his past, to assure himself of God's impotence and thus rid himself of any remaining remorse (955-62). Like his mistress, he has taken on God Himself, and can only be at peace with himself if he can be sure that God is dead.

Unfortunately, Mathan's antagonist is not much more savory. Like Mathan, Joad is clever, cunning, adept at handling people. (Note how he bolsters Abner's faith in act I, scene i, goading him, giving him hope, yet never telling him more than he absolutely must. Note likewise how he fans the hatred of the Levites in act IV, scene iii.) He frequently appears as ruthless in his methods, as devious, as cruel as Mathan. There are mitigating aspects and circumstances. Joad lies, but he does not twist values the way Mathan does. When he tells Athalie that the temple contains David's treasure, Athalie may consider that a lie, since there is no temporal treasure, but he is right: it contains Joas. It is Athalie's fault if her heart is too corrupt to capture the metaphor's important underlying truth.

Joad is more than a priest; he knows himself to be a prophet, a direct mouthpiece of God (84). He has no doubts therefore either about God or his righteousness and is arrogantly sure of having all the right answers to all questions, theological or other. Having seen with the eyes of God and spoken His words, he is far from free: that vision dictates a course of action; he can no longer be his own man. Though not a mindless puppet, he is a soldier committed to a cause which demands the total abnegation of self for the sake of a higher good. It is here that Joad truly becomes inhuman and unpalatable, for he serves a bloodthirsty God, one Who carries out the direst threats, and Joad revels in recollecting the bloody manifestations of His intervention. Phèdre's evil — and Athalie's to a lesser extent — has as an excuse her sensuality, her passions. Without that mitigation, the cruelty of Joad is bleakness itself. Senses are not only mitigations, they are cushions; only when totally devoid of personal feelings and passions can one be totally ferocious, and Joad is precisely that.

The main character in this play is God. He is the sole mover of everything, as Athalie herself recognizes in the end (1774). He has manipulated both Joad and Athalie, the incarnation of two forces dramatically united by Racine in the person of the child Joas, descendent of Ahab and Jezebel as much as of David. Athalie sees him first in her dream covered by priestly vestments; are these symbols of his purity, or are they, like Jezebel's make-up, merely the cover of his real being? As Athalie says (701–6), he has learned his lessons well and has been "infected" by Joad's bloody concept of God and his hatreds. Joas, in all his innocence, is blissfully unaware of his ability to hurt, and what begins as mere uneasiness turns into premonition and forboding when we combine what we see in him and what we hear Joad predict. Joas has in him the potential to effectuate God's promise; he also has the seed of violence so typical of his family, necessary adjunct to his fulfillment of Athalie's final curse.

This omnipresent and ambivalent God is drawn neither from the Old Testament nor from the New. If in *Esther* Racine has toned down the God of Vengeance by accentuating His more benevolent features, such is not the case in *Athalie.* This is a gory, unpleasant play, and if God is the main character, He is also the least likeable, His every manifestation and miracle being traced in blood. He is "faithful in all His threats" (112). From this God a promise and a threat are indistinguishable (1212). As the chorus asks, "How can one grant so much love with so much anger " (1214–15). To herald the coming of a God of Love, this play uses the words *avenge* and *vengeance* over thirty times (one-sixth of the frequency in all of Racine's works), and almost invariably with reference to God. The frequent references to love are no less revealing. Only three times is there mention of God's love, twice in instances of wishful thinking (768–69, 1229) and once when Joad announces that "Your God has rid Himself of His love for you" (1146). All other references are to the love one must have for Him, ironic echo of so many other Raci-

Athalie

nian situations where protagonists repeatedly asked for a love they did not know how to give.

Because His people have been perfunctory in their service, God has not manifested Himself in a long time; He *seems* absent, but only to the noninitiated. To those who can see, He is as active as ever, from the "miraculous" saving of Joas to the no less miraculous freeing of Abner and the dissolution of Athalie's army; it is His wisdom that makes forensic victors of the intellectually inferior Joas (II, vii) and Josabeth (III, iv). It might thus be argued that His overriding benevolence far outweighs His lust for blood. Such a view would not only excuse, it would legitimize the arrogance of Joad, the only protagonist with a view (however clouded) of the future and of God's design. This would remove all objections to his ruse concerning David's treasure; it would not make more palatable God's ruse — the dream that summons Athalie to the temple and to her destruction. It is difficult not to see Racine's return to the Jansenist fold in the depiction of this implacable divinity. When Achille mocked the thought of divine intervention, he obviously voiced views quite contrary to those of Joad; Achille saw wisdom only in the search for proper behavior regardless of the will of the gods; Joad, properly enlightened, sees that the divine plan will not suffer temporal intervention, and that all such intervention is as automatically bad as all obedience is certainly good. Ethics are no longer dictated at a human, personal level. Athalie cannot stop the cyclical move to salvation, the return to God of His people. The temple is located on the spot where Abraham almost sacrificed his son (a son necessary for the fulfillment of God's promise of eventual salvation) and though this temple is now surrounded by a great temporal power, Joad is not moved: God's will shall more than offset the seeming imbalance. That is what the profane cannot see or understand; God does not lie; nor does He reveal Himself to all.⁹ Only a select few can see Him; only they can hope to find a path to salvation; the rest is vanity.

For the love of humanity, this God demands that individuals be sacrificed at the human level. The stakes are high, and the just are used to suffering, but what of the sacrifice of principles and ethics, of the warping of basic notions of conduct? This play of reconciliation has little room for the human element. As the crisis is reached the human level is not so much transcended as it is obviated. The purification — by blood, a veritable blood bath of which we see only the central act — of Judah is an act of God in which human beings participate without full lucidity; not even Joad can fully grasp the implications of his holy mission. The sublime ceremony is not truly cathartic because it does not demand any human involvement — on stage or in the audience. It is an impressive ceremony, the enactment of a ritual that attempts to put us face to face with God; the view of this magnificent spectacle may find in its allegory many things, but not catharsis.[10] *Athalie,* representing an action at a level other than human, is imbued with neither tragic nor transcendental qualities.

That is both the greatness and the flaw of *Athalie.* Like M. Homais of Flaubert's *Madame Bovary,* I find myself torn between admiration for the style of the ceremony and blame for the ideas. Perhaps even closer to my views concerning this play are those enunciated by Camus in a totally different context. Like him, I cannot look with satisfaction upon a world in which "children suffer and die." The God of *Athalie* crushes man for the sake of mankind. I, like Camus, prefer a view that is optimistic for man;[11] not being eternal, I have relatively little use for an absolute such as "humanity."

To me, the sublime greatness of the play is in the formidable poetry, the creation of an unrelenting atmosphere meant to awe. The music of the lines, like the fanaticism of Joad, is supposed to recreate a biblical aura, and in this it succeeds. The nature of the place and the magnitude of the struggle do not allow for nuances of characterization. The result is a harsh, raucous canticle, one to a God I cannot love; but what music! The singers, like the actors, do not count. Only the work of God, the greater good, does. The human suffering therefore does not matter, and the fact that the victims do not deserve our pity is not even to the point. One can read or see *Phèdre* without believing in Venus and still be moved. Not so in *Athalie.* As Raymond Picard put it in his preface to the play, this "immense tragedy" is, "in every sense, the end of Racine."[12]

CHAPTER 14

Conclusion

DORANTE, in Molière's *Critique de L'Ecole des femmes,* says that the greatest rule of all is to please, and Uranie concurs when she points to the learned writers who, following all the rules, still manage to write plays that no one likes. Racine was of the same opinion and, in the dedicatory letter of *Andromaque,* he said no less: "We, who work to please the public, no longer need ask savants if we are working according to rules. The sovereign rule is to please your Royal Highness." As he frequently repeated afterward, his main objective was "plaire et toucher." To accomplish this he saw the need to rid plays of all that was "useless and languishing," that is to say, all that was not to the point. His plays, characters, and actions are therefore logical and probable and require little or no exterior propulsion once the a priori are accepted. Rather than filling a play with a multitude of events, he concentrated our attention on a minute psychological vivisection. In so doing he deliberately turned his back on Corneille's predilection for the astounding truth to champion the cause of verisimilitude: only that which is *vraisemblable* can touch, the extraordinary verging on the absurd being a barrier to credibility and involvement. In this rarefied air of psychological verisimilitude, bombastic tirades and dramatic histrionics are out of place. If a drama is to be the representation of souls in flux, anything that might distract must be banished. Thus, plastic details were kept to a minimum, and those absolutely necessary to the plot were relegated offstage lest their physical aspects lack verisimilitude and detract from the atmosphere. The three famous unities thus ceased to be fetters and became intrinsic parts of the internal structure of the crises. Even peripeteias were made to work toward this end; whereas Corneille had seen them as ups and downs of fortune that could complicate a plot, Racine used them in a purer, Aristotelian sense as inversions of the expected consequence of a word or act; Racinian peripeteias add an ironic dimension to the tragedy, they heighten the tension but never complicate the single, simple action involving a minimum of protagonists who come face to face with their fate in a specific place, at a specific time.

In a brief biblical, mythological, or historical anecdote, Racine was thus able to find a human crisis implying a universal moral. Not content with the stylization of such a situation, he makes us participate in the suffering of individuals, balancing the sins of some with the virtues of others or revealing such a division within a single heart. Most great Racinian characterizations are marked by insoluble inner contradictions, which are exacerbated by the struggle between the being and his destiny, itself frequently interiorized as in the cases of Oreste and Phèdre. If a single axis were to be determined for this struggle it would have to be that of the interplay of intelligence and passion. Though possessed by irresistible passions, the Racinian characters never forget their obligations to themselves — lucidity and reason remain to torture them — but they are simply unable to fulfill them. The resulting shame and self-loathing contribute no little to their recourse to desperate measures. To these *dégradés* all is fair in the perfidious war of love. In these visual and verbal confrontations that are the Racinian scenes, everything betrays these ensnared victims of fate and of themselves, and exposes them to the judgments they most fear: "Everything betrays us: voice, silence, eyes; and ill-covered flames burst out only more fiercely," says Oreste (575-76), and Néron implies no less when he threatens Junie: "J'entendrai des regards que vous croirez muets" (682).[1]

Predetermined by heredity, these characters are not free; the grandeur of the drama is that they act as though they were, judging themselves responsible. Evil is visited on them AND within them, and they cannot put to sleep that gnawing consiousness and conscience, however much they might like to. In the clutches of cruel gods, they aspire to be good and must succumb to evil. "In one sense Oedipus suffers forces he can neither control nor understand, the puppet of fate; yet at the same time he wills and intelligently intends his every move."[2] In Sophocles — and in Corneille — one might see such autonomy in the actualization of an essence; not so in Racine, where the struggle is centered on the acceptance of an

Conclusion

essence already given. The grandeur of these human beings lies elsewhere: "The heroes of Racine who affirm their responsibility affirm as well their freedom. One cannot be guilty without the possibility of not being so. Now, the Racinian character frequently has an acute awareness of his responsibility."[3] The outcome of the game of life may be settled in advance, but, as Achille sees it, what matters is how he plays that game.

Though the nature and scope of this study have not allowed me to give full due to the poetry of Racine, a final word must be said concerning its illuminating quality — did not the Greeks consider tragedy as illumination? It is the nature of poetry to make something happen. That truism must be juxtaposed with another one: "Language is the light that dissipates doubts,"[4] though in Racine language is frequently a vehicle of deception and the word only a sometime ally of poetry. In this peerless poetry, impossible to render into English, the main purpose of the word is to evoke the unspoken — "Roxane vit le prince" — that which is best unexplained, what must be grasped beyond mere meaning or mere reality. Here agin we come face to face with Philip Butler's fine statement: "What Racine reaches for, beyond the confusing world of reality, is truth."

Notes and References

Preface

1. For the sake of consistency and clarity I have kept the French version of Racine's names (Néron, Alexandre), but have used the English forms for historical and mythological figures not in the plays (Seneca, Augustus).
2. *Two Centuries of French Literature* (New York: McGraw-Hill, 1970), p. 94.
3. *Autonomie de Racine* (Paris: Corti, 1967). It is impossible in these few pages to do justice to this important background material, and I urge the reader to consult the works mentioned in section I. C. of the Bibliography.
4. (Cambridge: University Press, 1967).

Chapter One

1. The Bourgogne troupe was considered first in tragedy, Molière's group in comedy; since tragedy was considered the superior genre, the prestige went to the first.
2. *Oeuvres* (Paris: Seuil, 1963), p. 862. The translation — like all subsequent ones — is my own.
3. There have been only four performances at the Comédie Française since 1700, none in this century.
4. *La Carrière de Jean Racine* (Paris: Gallimard, 1961), pp. 156–61.
5. Little by little the city was following the court whose infatuation with things of Turkish flavor had been set off by the visit of a lavish legation from Turkey to the court of Louis XIV.
6. Among these were the niece of Mazarin, the Duchess of Bouillon and her brother, the Duke of Nevers, and many others who, like them, were outcasts from the court surrounded by rivals and detractors of Racine, whose pro-court attitude was a thorn in their side.
7. *Aspects de Racine* (Paris: Nizet, 1954), p. 99.
8. Op. cit., pp. 289–312.
9. An ironic stroke of fate occurred in 1726 when the house of Valincour, successor of Racine at the academy and historiographer of the king after Racine, burned to the ground and with it Racine's entire work as historiographer.

10. Op. cit., p. 315.
11. Ibid., p. 395.
12. On one occasion the glittering audience included the king and queen of England.
13. Not until 1721 did Paris get to see *Esther*. Performed without music the play was but a shadow of what Racine had meant it to be, and it failed miserably.
14. Op. cit., pp. 422–28.
15. Ibid., p. 465.

Chapter Two

1. *La Crise de la conscience européenne* (Paris: Boivin, 1935).
2. *"Polyeucte" and "Le Menteur"* (New York: Dell, 1963), p. 24.
3. *The Idea of a Theater* (New York: Doubleday, 1953), p. 61. My emphasis.
4. It is beyond the scope of this brief study to give an adequate description of this background. I refer the reader to section 1. C. of the Bibliography. The Lough volume is particularly good for a first acquaintance.
5. *La Tragédie* (Paris: Colin, 1964), p. 20.
6. Ibid., pp. 26–27.
7. *L'Oeil vivant* (Paris: Gallimard, 1961), p. 16.
8. *The Birth of Tragedy* (New York: Doubleday, 1956), pp. 51–52.
9. The hit of the 1971–72 season at the Comédie Française was "Richard III," and I consider Margaret Rawlings one of the great Phèdres of our time.
10. Lucien Goldmann, "Structure de la tragédie racinienne," in *Le Théâtre tragique,* ed. Jean Jacquot (Paris: CNRS, 1962), p. 256.
11. "A Minimal Definition of Seventeenth-century Tragedy," *French Studies* 10 (1956), 305.
12. Fergusson, p. 61.
13. For a brief discussion of the unity of action in *Le Cid,* see my *Pierre Corneille* (New York: Twayne, 1972), pp. 57 sq.
14. Odette de Mourgues, *Autonomie de Racine* (Paris: Corti, 1967), p. 24.

Chapter Three

1. Between 1681 and 1684 the Comédie Française tried several times to revive it, but with little success; the same troupe performed it eight times during the eighteenth century and only five times since.
2. "Racine's *Thébaïde:* An Analysis." *French Studies* 13 (July 1959), 200.
3. *Racine* (Paris: Gallimard, 1947), p. 238.

4. *Aspects of Racinian Tragedy* (Toronto: Toronto University Press, 1956), p. 52.

5. For a fuller treatment of this aspect of time in Racine, see the chapter on *Bérénice* or "Time in *Bérénice*" by Sandra Soares and Claude Abraham, *Romance Notes* 15 (1973), 104–109.

6. *A New View of the Plays of Racine* (London: Macmillan, 1948), p. 5.

7. "Racine's *Thébaïde*," p. 205. Though Racine left it out of this play, another ironic twist must have been obvious to a public aware of the entire legend: by causing the death of Antigone, Créon fulfilled the first oracle, but also set in motion another curse: Antigone, protected by the gods, would have to be avenged by the fall of Thebes itself.

8. "A Note on Racine's *Thébaïde*," *FS* 10 (1956), 20–31.

9. *Essai d'exégèse racinienne* (Paris: Nizet, 1956), p. 48.

10. *Sur Racine* (Paris: Seuil, 1963), p. 69.

11. Brody, p. 207.

12. Brody, p. 211. Brody particularly objects to the following: "Creon's tragic illumination is trumped up and inadequately prepared. The Creon-Antigone-Haemon love triangle is badly out of tune with the terrible tenor of the rest of the drama."

13. Martin Turnell, *Jean Racine Dramatist* (London: Hamish Hamilton, 1972), p. 44.

14. *Histoire de la littérature française du XVIIe siècle* (Paris: Del Duca, 1968), IV, 307.

15. Axiane thinks that she loves glory most, but eventually (IV, i) she realizes and admits that Porus is more important to her, and that her espousal of glory was merely a reflection of his ideas.

Chapter Four

1. *Essai d'exégèse racinienne,* pp. 78–79.

2. *Etudes sur le temps humain* (Paris: Plon, 1950), p. 105.

3. For example, see the analysis of *Horace* in my *Corneille,* especially p. 61, and contrast the cited examples with *Alexandre,* lines 1001, 1500, etc.

4. Instances of such balancing are too numerous to be discussed here. See, for example, lines 122, 540, 542, 544, or the frequently cited line that so perfectly describes Hermione as "ever ready to leave, and ever remaining" (131).

5. The second hemistich of l. 1568 ("et suis-je Oreste enfin") is ambiguous. It has often been translated as "am I indeed Oreste?" Written as it is, without a comma, it could just as readily mean "am I Oreste at last?", i.e., am I now what I was destined to be all along?

6. Unlike Andromaque, Pyrrhus would rather forget a victory and a night which, "far more cruel than we, incited us to murder" (211-12). Andromaque sees that same night as one during which "Pyrrhus, with blazing eyes, entered by the light of our burning palaces, and making his way over the bodies of our dead brothers, covered with blood, incited to fresh slaughter" (999-1002). By the same token, Hermione, in spite of her need for Oreste — or because she resents that need — never misses an opportunity to make him suffer. See, for instance, the ferocity of her tirade when, having exposed her vulnerability in demanding Pyrrhus' death, and Oreste having demurred, she rejects Oreste, ending with a savage "I would rather die with him than live with you" (1247-48).

7. *Jean Racine: un itinéraire poétique* (Montréal: Presses de l'Université de Montréal, 1970), p. 50.

8. Op. cit., p. 81.

9. "The 'Innocent Stratagème' of Racine's *Andromaque*," *French Review* 48 (February, 1975), 562.

10. Ibid., p. 563.

11. *Essai d'exégèse,* p. 76.

Chapter Five

1. Adam, IV, 324.

2. Pierre Clarac, *L'Age classique* (Paris: Arthaud, 1969), p. 244.

3. While most of these writings are of interest only to the student of literary history, at least one of them defies that generalization. Jean Dubu, in "Racine, les plaideurs et les juges," *Napoli, Instituto Orientale, Annali, Sezione Romanza* 11 (1969), 3-32, masterfully integrates what at first seem like historical and sociological bits of trivia with genuine critical insight to paint a meaningful picture.

4. During the eighteenth century it was performed 507 times at the Comédie Française. Only *Phèdre,* with 424 performances, came close.

5. Cf., for instance, lines 154, 368, 601 of *Les Plaideurs* with lines 35, 227, 266 of *Le Cid. Horace* and *Polyeucte* also get their fair share of barbs. However, it must be remembered that not even Corneille could resist the temptation to parody his own most grandiloquent lines (see my *Corneille,* pp. 81-82).

6. The best of these studies is by Nathan Gross, "Racine's Debt to Aristophanes," *Comparative Literature* 17 (1965), 209-24.

7. Aristophanes' comedies rely heavily on verbal fantasy, but that is the part most readily lost as the play crosses linguistic and cultural barriers. Racine, quite properly, substituted a new brand, wholly French — though indebted to the verve of the *comedia dell'arte* — and unfortunately equally untranslatable.

8. Some have seen in Perrin Dandin a challenge to Molière, who had

Notes and References

just created his *George Dandin,* but the more likely source for this character is the Perrin Dendin of Rabelais' *Tiers Livre,* who is also an inveterate trial addict, judging more cases than can be tried in several provinces.

9. For instance, at one point L'Intimé claims to give a copy of a summons to Chicanneau; but he has already (he claims) given it to Isabelle and has only the original left; in this case, the impasselike nature of the situation, glossed over by all concerned, only adds to the comic effect.

10. Praising his wife and older virtues, Dandin points with pride to her frugality: she never returns from the courthouse without at least a towel to show for her effort. This allusion to a miserly woman of Racine's time accused of stealing the napkins from the courthouse buffet, funny in itself, must have been even more so to those aware of the parallel, but its very timeliness prevents it today from having the effect it once did.

11. *L'Age classique,* p. 244.

12. *La Fantaisie verbale et le comique* (Paris: Colin, 1957), pp. 294-97. This union of the physical with the verbal is just as evident at the beginning of the "symphony": when Petit Jean is told not to stand so stiffly during his tirade, he begins to wildly wave his arms, setting the farcical mood for the rest of the scene.

13. Enhancing the shock of the word with its alliteration is the definition: Pimbesche is a scornful way to refer to an overbearing and impertinent woman.

14. When Chicanneau speaks of perverting justice (168-75) the satire is more against the system than against him, but his own sense of values is nevertheless criticized (182-86).

15. "*Les Plaideurs* and the Racinian Canon," *Modern Language Notes* 80 (1966), 334, 320.

Chapter Six

1. *Essai d'exégèse,* p. 107.

2. See Jean Rohou, "Etude d'un personnage racinien: les complaisances du vertueux Burrhus," *Information Littéraire* 26 (1974), 45.

3. I view Néron's decision to divorce his wife (chosen by Agrippine) as another aspect of his rejection of his mother. To him the wife is but one more reminder of maternal domination.

4. In the theater of Racine only "utility words" are used more frequently than the verb *voir,* to see; only *seigneur* and *coeur,* "lord" and "heart," occur more frequently than *oeil* and *yeux,* "eye(s)." See Bryant C. Freeman and Alan Batson, *Concordance du théâtre et des poésies de Jean Racine* (Ithaca: Cornell University Press, 1968).

5. This line, already quoted, is one of many such individually perfectly balanced lines in which, as Fergusson puts it, "one feels the logical form of thesis and antithesis, the tragic split between reason and passion" (*The*

Idea of a Theater, p. 66). There are, of course, equally striking examples of turmoil, revealed by the very opposite technique of radical breaks in metrics; see, for instance, 460-61 or 572.

6. Starobinski, pp. 85-86. For a perspicacious treatment of the importance of vision in *Britannicus,* see Jules Brody, "Les Yeux de César: The Language of Vision in *Britannicus,*" in *Studies in Honor of Morris Bishop,* ed. J.-J. Demorest (Ithaca: Cornell University Press, 1963), pp. 185-201.

7. It could be argued that Néron is aware of its transparency and enjoys the added discomfort of a comprehending interlocutor's impotence.

8. Lapp, pp. 69-70.

9. The priestesses of Vesta were the keepers of the eternal flame; after his death, Augustus was raised to the rank of god.

10. Physicality has two dangers: it is difficult to portray or relate on stage, and the slightest accident at a performance can lead to laughter, as overacting can lead to melodrama and bathos. Nevertheless, Racine knew how to use physical elements, though he has been frequently criticized for lack of such knowledge. Scene iii of the last act has often been viewed as padding, to allow Britannicus to go offstage and be killed, but it is much more than that: during this scene Agrippine reveals her tenacious belief in her power, Junie her more lucid fatalism. The entire scene, in the way Agrippine's ever-rising song of triumph is cut short by the noise off stage and Burrhus' rushing in with the news of Néron's total emancipation via murder, is a fabulous *coup de théâtre.*

11. "Racine rival de Corneille," *Romanic Review* 66 (January, 1975), 30.

Chapter Seven

1. Racine was no less inventive when it came to the lovelorn Antiochus, the third member of the play's erotic triangle, a faithful and unhappy suitor of Bérénice. There was indeed an Antiochus, king of Commagene, but by 79 A.D. his domain had become a Roman province, and the old king, having given some help to the conquerors, was allowed to die peacefully in Rome. There is no indication that he ever met Berenice.

2. In *Bérénice* their role is particularly restricted. Whenever more than one principal is on stage, the confidants remain silent (with only two minor exceptions). They are entirely excluded from the last two scenes.

3. P. 133.

4. Like Rodrigue and Chimène, Titus and Bérénice *must* be exemplary. Were Titus to agree to Bérénice's selfish demands, how long could it be before Rome would mock them? More important still, how long before she "would blush at the memory of his cowardice" (1403) and drag the idyllic union into a hell of mutual recriminations?

5. See, for instance, Raymond Picard, *Oeuvres complètes de Racine* (Paris: Gallimard, 1950), I, 457. If one were to speak of illumination, of secular grace, it would have to refer to Bérénice, not Titus. He knows what he must do from the start. His vacillation is not one of ignorance but of doubt as to his strength. The peripeteias deal with that brinksmanship, but perhaps even more with his efforts to infect Bérénice with his outlook, which alone can save their love.

6. *Aspects,* p. 21. However, it is important not to see the ending as some sort of political resolution, a Cornelian sacrifice of love to regal duty. By putting them in a certain position, history forces the lovers to make a decision, but the real reason for the decision lies in their agreement as to the only way to save their love from the banalities that would inevitably engulf it were they to reject the challenge.

7. As has been noted before, Racine seems to take pleasure in flirting with disaster. Here he comes close to melodrama; in the opening lines of act V, scene v, he comes dangerously close to comedy, and only a sensitive actress can keep that scene in the intensely tragic domain.

8. Michael Edwards, *La Tragédie racinienne* (Paris: Pensée Universelle, 1972), p. 174.

9. The eyes play as large a role in *Bérénice* as in the previous plays, and Antiochus, who cannot expect words of consolation, seeks other signals of understanding: "I see that your heart secretly approves of me, I see that I am heard . . ." (225-26).

10. As I have stated above, Antiochus is somewhat reluctant, but he has already anticipated Bérénice's last words in making his stand. His final "Alas" is not in response to her last few words, but to the full implications of the "tableau."

11. For a brief yet clear analysis of Racine's technique of linking scenes, see Lapp, pp. 117-19.

12. The following pages are extracted from Sandra Soares and Claude Abraham, "Time in *Bérénice*", pp. 104-9.

13. Grammatically the present tense of the French "je la vois" is difficult to translate, but it is important to convey the idea that Titus does not wish to consider that period irrevocably in the past.

14. No other play comes close in that respect: *Bajazet,* the nearest rival, uses the word 23 times, and *Mithridate,* 22. In fact, only two other plays use the word more frequently than this first act of *Bérénice.* For concentrated use, only the last act of this play, with 10 occurrences, comes close. For a complete breakdown, see Freeman and Batson, passim.

Chapter Eight

1. *Oeuvres de Racine,* p. 523.
2. Ibid.

3. *Essai,* p. 153.
4. Mourgues, p. 42.
5. Ibid., p. 30.
6. Early in the play we learn that Bajazet must remove whatever doubt his ambiguous words have left in Roxane's mind (330). In that sense the three middle acts and much of the last deal with his decision to be frank and open at any cost.
7. In a world in which people try to fathom minds, to read thoughts, to guess at feelings in expressions and in each other's eyes, this is most important: not even expressions are reliable, and one must frequently fall back on trickery to catch people off guard (as in the case of Roxane telling Atalide that she will obey the order to have Bajazet killed; as Atalide's reaction shows, some people can hide their feelings, and others cannot).
8. *Histoire,* IV, 349.
9. Edwards, p. 184.
10. Ronald Tobin, "The Too-Faithful Reflection: Self-Hatred in the Tragedies of Racine," *Esprit Créateur* 8, no. 2 (Summer 1968), 107. "Purity" may be debatable, the rest not. She claims to have reached the "apex of glory" (1533), but she cannot believe this while striving for the elusive wedlock. It might be observed that while her savagery hardly conforms to French concepts of femininity, her desire for matrimony definitely is more in keeping with the thinking of Versailles than of Constantinople.
11. As she vacillates between love and hatred, gentle persuasion and threats (512–68), she constantly switches between *tu* and *vous.* The cajoling slave can say "je sens que je vous aime," but the rejected sultana will interrupt an insincere declaration with a brutally scornful "Ne m'importune plus." This is again the case in their last confrontation. She reproaches him for repaying her love, her confidence, by "feigning a love you (*vous*) did not feel," but when he interjects a most unheroic "Who, I, Madam?" her tone changes to a terse "Oui, toi" (1480–81).
12. Roxane, like Bérénice, tries to legitimize her illusions, accepting anything that will keep alive a hope that lucidity would kill. As long as Bérénice blinded herself to the obvious, as long as she thought herself the victim of some injustice — even one perpetrated by the man she loved — she could hope for a reversal. Once fully grasped, the truth killed action, hope, and willful flights to inauthenticity. In that respect Roxane walks in her footsteps.
13. *Essai d'exégèse,* pp. 142–43.

Chapter Nine

1. The deliberately redundant line could be considered the thematic condensation of the entire play. It might also be pointed out in this connec-

Notes and References

tion that few plays have as many threatened, contemplated, or attempted suicides, and that seldom has there been a "hero" more willing to hurt the ones he loves.

2. Edwards, p. 203. This duality is interestingly presented at a lexical level as well: the young lovers being forced to lie, the word *secret* and its derivatives are used more frequently in *Mithridate* than in any other play (as is to be expected, *Bajazet* and *Britannicus* are close competitors); but since they are "innocent" liars and need feel no guilt, the word *cacher* ("to hide") is used relatively little; it will be used twice as often in *Phèdre*.

3. Entire phrases are plucked out of Corneille; cf., for instance, 1595 of *Mithridate* and 277 of *Le Cid*.

4. The sentence that begins at line 9 with "Thus the king..." does not find its verb until the telling *rejet* "dies" four lines later, a minor *coup de théâtre* in itself. The process is repeated with equal effectiveness some lines later, when Xipharès mentions "that beautiful Monime" and digresses until an impatient intervention by his interlocutor brings forth the simple "I love her" at the hemistich (35).

5. "For the first and last time ... I tell you, my Lord, never to tell you again, my honor recalls me [to my duty] as it drags me to the altar, where I will pledge you my eternal silence. I hear you sigh, but such is my misery: I am not yours, but your father's." After the strong antithetical lines that begin the tirade, the powerful union of words as in line 697 (*rappelle* and *entraîne* tying "honor" to "altar"), or the surprise of the strange vows to be sworn at the nuptial altar, the tableau is completed by a final telling set of dichotomies — his sighs, her misery; their love, her obligation.

6. *Manuel dramatique* (Paris: Painparré, 1822), p. 58.

7. "La Structure sociale de l'autorité dans le théâtre de Racine." *Cahiers Raciniens* 30 (1971), 37-38.

8. Here again we are dealing with a Cornelian commonplace, of youngsters giving a lesson in generosity to their elders, as seen in *Le Cid* (1061-70), *Horace,* and especially *Nicomède* (see my *Corneille,* pp. 102-9). Like Nicomède's father Prusias, Mithridate — who decided to marry Monime only when his earthier propositions were rejected — must learn to sacrifice not himself but that which is base in himself; whereas Prusias is incapable of this leap to generosity, Mithridate ultimately saves his essence thanks to the contagious generosity of his son. Like *Bérénice,* this is the story of a search for an essence by the transcendence of all that is imperfect in the human heart.

9. *Histoire,* IV, 353.

10. N.-M. Bernardin, "Mithridate," *Revue des Cours et Conférences* 9, no. 1 (1900), 84.

11. Lapp, p. 48.

Chapter Ten

1. Robert Kemp, "Chronique théâtrale," *Temps,* 16 May, 1938.
2. Under stress, Eriphile frequently becomes irrational, betraying a lack of coherence and self-control which Racine will so masterfully exploit in his next play.
3. Raymond Picard, "Racine Among Us," *Yale French Studies* 5 (1950), 45. Embodiment of discord, this Iphigénie is as instrumental as her counterpart in conveying the "sacred" message of this tragedy.
4. Russel Pfohl, *Racine's "Iphigénie"* (Geneva: Droz, 1974), p. 118.
5. For a study of the gradual evolvement of this canon, see my *Corneille,* pp. 114-49.
6. Gutwirth, p. 69.
7. *Expliquez-moi Iphigénie* (Paris: Foucher, 1963), p. 38. To grasp the intensity of her carnal side, see her declaration to Achille (III, vi).
8. Pfohl, p. 116.
9. Lapp, p. 30.
10. Unlike Euripides' altar, that of Racine serves a dual purpose and is thus simultaneously a symbol of death and of love. Much of the irony is derived from this coexistence, as each reference to the altar means love to Iphigénie, death to those who know better.
11. To situate the time, reference is made to the babe Orestes; who can fail to cringe when Iphigénie, to console her mother, tells her to find solace and joy in him (1661-62)?
12. For a thorough discussion of this element, see John Lapp, "Time, Space, and Symbol in *Iphigénie,*" *PMLA* 66 (1951), 1023-32.
13. For a full discussion of these points, see Hubert, pp. 187 sq. As he points out, the truly tragic element of any play is the sacrifice of life to an abstraction — and has there ever been an emptier one? The struggles here are less between individuals than between rival abstractions. Having sacrificed their humanity, these "heroes" will deserve the endings that the future holds in store for them.
14. Pfohl, p. 200.
15. Ibid., p. 225.

Chapter Eleven

1. Lapp, p. 33.
2. Thierry Maulnier, *Lecture de Phèdre* (Paris: Gallimard, 1967), pp. 39-40. This solitude, as Maulnier points out, is dramatically made manifest by the silence of her antagonists: her confessions and declarations are veritable monologues barely punctuated by a few short interjections which she sweeps aside "violently or tenderly" with an "invincible superiority" (pp. 40-41).

3. Ronald Tobin, *Racine and Seneca* (Chapel Hill: University of North Carolina Press, 1971), p. 143.
4. It is important not to confuse regret with remorse. Early in the play Phèdre is ready to die, and on seeing the sun thinks of shady forests ... in which she can furtively watch Hippolyte (176-78); at the height of her feelings of guilt and shame, her greatest sorrow is voiced when she laments the fact that she has been unable to enjoy the fruit of her dark crime (1291-92).
5. Like Monime of *Mithridate* (1106-8) — but far more vibrantly — she sees in the son a flawless reincarnation of what the father once was.
6. "Innocent Hippolyte," *French Review* 43 (April, 1970), 775-82.
7. A tangential paradox becomes apparent here: once tamed, will not Hippolyte begin to resemble his philandering father? No less paradoxical (though logical, since Aricie and Thésée are of the same monstrous lineage) is the fact that Thésée too likes his loves virginal and, having debased them by his possession, abandons them. How would the Aricie-Hippolyte love have fared had he survived?
8. Just as the gods belong to the dramatis personae, so their entire universe is the stage for the action. The sea and the forests, the sun and Hades are not frontiers, but parts of the locus.
9. Hubert, p. 203.
10. The word *monstre(s)* occurs thirty times in Racine, eighteen in *Phèdre* alone. Phèdre uses it five times, twice to describe herself; Hippolyte also uses it five times, once to describe his Amazon mother, four times literally; Thésée uses it twice literally, once to refer to his son; Théramène uses it twice literally, but Aricie uses it in a double entendre, accusing Phèdre too ambiguously for a dull-witted Thésée.
11. Gutwirth, p. 140. Another echo might be evoked: Phèdre, like Neptune's monster, succumbs in her successful attempt to destroy Hippolyte.
12. Obvious, but not overly simple: Phèdre's father represents wisdom, yet resides in Hades; her mother, representing lust, is the daughter of the Sun.
13. These notions are based on the masterful stage directions of Jean-Louis Barrault in his edition of *Phèdre* (Paris: Seuil, 1946).
14. Starobinski, p. 20.
15. Nathan Edelman, *The Eye of the Beholder* (Baltimore: Johns Hopkins University Press, 1974), p. 141.
16. *Racine* (Paris: Revue Française, 1935), p. 25.

Chapter Twelve

1. For the longest time, the Comédie Française did not even have an orchestra pit; no conductor, from backstage, could keep track simultaneously of his orchestra and of the chorus on stage.

2. At the 1972 Festival du Marais I saw a performance of *Esther* in which the gestures and many of the spoken lines were so wooden as to verge on the comic.
3. *Aspects de Racine,* p. 223.
4. The prologue, containing flattery for the king, has little to do with the play itself which was already finished, and whose roles were already distributed when it was discovered that Mme de Caylus, an adult inmate of Saint-Cyr, had no part; the prologue — a purely occasional piece — was added to allow Mme de Caylus to participate in the festivities.
5. Lapp, p. 32.
6. Edwards, pp. 286-89.
7. *Essai,* pp. 230-31.
8. In plays such as *Bérénice, Mithridate, Phèdre,* the poetry is frequently forgotten, taken for granted as spectators and readers alike fall under the spell of the dramatist. In *Esther,* where the characters are monofaceted, the action obvious, nothing detracts from the lyricism, from the music of the lines which rivals Moreau's music.

Chapter Thirteen
1. At the end of the play Joas is anointed as king. Both Messiah (Hebrew) and Christ (Greek) mean "anointed."
2. Hubert, p. 243.
3. Once Joad sees the future, it poisons his present; he knows exactly how his beloved Joas will repay his vigilence (1325). Only for the truly omniscient (God) do all periods of time coexist.
4. The private property of Louis XIV, *Athalie* was not performed in Paris until after his death and then without the choruses and music, therefore only with mild success. (Even Saint-Cyr and the provincial convents where *Athalie* was performed had the good sense to leave in the choruses). Only on the few occasions where it was selected for performances at great official functions did the play get its just, spectacular treatment. For one such occasion (1786) Haydn wrote a new score for the solo parts. Throughout the nineteenth century there were new productions of *Athalie* with new scores (Boieldieu, Gossec, Cohen, etc.), many of these produced with great pomp at the Opéra, but until modern times the Comédie Française insisted on performing the truncated version.
5. As in *Esther,* the number of lines is a bad indication of the importance of the chanted part; the chorus' lines are relatively few in number, yet they take up nearly one-third of the performance time.
6. "Racine mélode," *Mélanges offerts à Georges Mongrédien* (Paris: d'Argences, 1974), p. 410.
7. Maulnier, p. 259.
8. Without this belief, the play loses all sense, as it did for D'Alembert

who could feel no interest either for Athalie "who is a nasty bitch," nor for Joad "who is an insolent priest" (Letter to Voltaire, December 11, 1769), Voltaire saw in the play a masterpiece of the human mind because Racine had held his interest without a love intrigue, relying only on a priest, an old woman, and a child, but he also considered this *tour de force* a "masterpiece of fanaticism" (Letter to Cideville, May 20, 1761).

9. Thus Jansenism can be viewed as tinging the texture of the entire play. It is easy (though not very fruitful) to see in the small handful of Jews remaining loyal to the true faith a representation of the Jansenists.

10. His notes on Aristotle show that Racine considered catharsis an emotional rather than a moral cleansing.

11. *Essai* (Paris: Gallimard, 1965), p. 372.

12. *Oeuvres,* p. 870.

Conclusion

1. *Entendre* meaning both "hear" and "understand," the line's strength and Néron's cruelty are conveyed by a play on words: "I will hear/understand glances that you consider mute."

2. Fergusson, p. 30.

3. Jacques Scherer, "La Liberté du personnage racinien," *Le Théâtre tragique,* ed. J. Jacquot (Paris: CNRS, 1962), p. 265.

4. Jacques Guicharnaud, *Seventeenth-century French Drama* (N.Y.: Modern Library, 1967), p. xx.

Selected Bibliography

BACKGROUND MATERIALS AND GENERAL STUDY AIDS

A. Bibliographies

CIORANESCU, ALEXANDRE. *Bibliographie de la littérature française du dix-septième siècle.* 3 vols. Paris: CNRS, 1965-66. The most complete of the available bibliographies, very useful in spite of some errors and omissions.

CABEEN, DAVID C., and JULES BRODY. *A Critical Bibliography of French Literature, Volume III: The Seventeenth Century.* Syracuse: Syracuse University Press, 1961. This volume, edited by Nathan Edelman, while far from complete should be the most useful to the general reader insofar as it judiciously comments on the items selected for inclusion. Sadly out of date it must be used with its forthcoming supplement or with Gravit et al.

GRAVIT, FRANCIS W., et al. *Bibliography of French Seventeenth-Century Studies.* Bloomington: Indiana University, 1953-68; Washington, D. C.: George Washington University, 1969-71; and Fort Collins: Colorado State University, 1972 to date. Although there has been a change in the editorship this annual bibliography, published for the Modern Language Association French Group III, is still called the "Gravit Bibliography." While it is not truly critical, it is carefully annotated and, for the general reader, the most useful supplement to the "Cabeen."

KLAPP, OTTO. *Bibliographie d'histoire littéraire française.* Frankfurt: Klostermann, 1956 to date. Appearing every two years this is the most complete of the periodic bibliographies.

B. Dictionaries

DUBOIS, J., and R. LAGANE. *Dictionnaire de la langue française classique.* Paris: Belin, 1960. Indispensable, especially for the understanding of archaisms.

GRENTE, CARDINAL GEORGES. *Dictionnaire des lettres françaises. Le dix-septième siècle.* Paris: Fayard, 1954. First-rate for biographical sketches with longer articles for selected topics.

C. Literary, Historical, Social, and Political Background

In view of the wide selection available only books in English are suggested here.

BENICHOU, PAUL. *Man and Ethics; Studies in French Classicism.* Garden City: Doubleday, 1971. Translation by E. Hughes of a brilliant work.
BRERETON, GEOFFREY. *French Tragic Drama in the Sixteenth and Seventeenth Centuries.* London: Methuen, 1974. Thorough, eminently readable synthesis.
CRUICKSHANK, JOHN. *French Literature and Its Background. II: 17th Century.* Oxford: Oxford University Press, 1968. The work of a large team of scholars; the value of its intelligent insights is enhanced by chronological charts, synoptic tables, and a comprehensive index.
HOWARD, W. D. *The Seventeenth Century.* London: Nelson, 1965. Very learned, yet eminently readable book on life and letters.
LANCASTER, HENRY CARRINGTON. *A History of French Dramatic Literature in the 17th Century.* 9 vols. Baltimore: Johns Hopkins University Press, 1929-42. Reprinted in 1952 with corrections, this is a monumental work, an indispensable mine of information.
LOUGH, JOHN. *An Introduction to Seventeenth-Century France.* New York: McKay, 1969. Unpretentious. As good an introduction as one could wish for.
MOORE, W. G. *The Classical Drama of France.* Oxford: Oxford Univ. Press, 1971. Uneven work by one of the most astute scholars in the field who tries to do too much in too few pages.
YARROW, P. J. *A Literary History of France. Vol. II: The Seventeenth Century.* New York: Barnes and Noble, 1967. Though without the broad base of Cruickshank this is a fine book, perhaps the best of its kind in English, with a superlative section on theater.

PRIMARY SOURCES

OEuvres complètes, ed. by Raymond Picard. Paris: Gallimard, 1966-68. This two-volume edition in the Pléiade collection is the most complete and accurate of the modern ones.

Racine's sublime poetry has successfully defied the efforts of the best translators. There is no truly satisfactory English version of his theater. The following are therefore subject to caution.

The Complete Plays of Jean Racine, transl. by Samuel Solomon. New York: Modern Library, 1969. 2 vols. A noble and sometimes successful effort.

Jean Racine. Five Plays, transl. by Kenneth Muir. New York: Hill and Wang, 1960. *Andromaque, Bérénice, Britannicus, Phèdre,* and *Athalie.* Fairly satisfactory and, in my opinion, the best.

Phèdre, transl. by Margaret Rawlings. New York: Dutton, 1963. From the dramatic point of view a superb translation, but the Muir remains my choice overall.

SECONDARY SOURCES

It is impossible to list even a significant fraction of the legion of studies dealing with Racine. (Cioranescu alone lists well over 1300 items all of which appeared before 1960.) I have therefore listed here only some of the better recent studies in English, giving preference to the more general ones.

BRERETON, GEOFFREY. *Jean Racine.* London: Cassell, 1951. Best biography in English.

CLARK, A. F. B. *Jean Racine.* Cambridge: Harvard Univ. Press, 1939. Solid and sound but rather unimaginative.

FRANCE, PETER. *Racine's Rhetoric.* Oxford: Clarendon Press, 1965. Penetrating look into Racine's use of rhetorical elements.

KNIGHT, R. C., ed. *Racine.* London: MacMillan, 1969. Very useful collection of articles, many previously unavailable in English.

LAPP, JOHN C. *Aspects of Racinian Tragedy.* Toronto: Toronto Univ. Press, 1956. Thematic analyses. One of the finest books ever written on Racine in any language.

MOURGUES, ODETTE DE. *Racine or the Triumph of Relevance.* Cambridge: Cambridge Univ. Press, 1967. Superb book in every way; shows, as the French title indicates *(Autonomie de Racine),* that Racine is coherent and must be viewed as an entity, not vivisected for anachronistic and overspecialized "fireworks".

ORGEL, VERA. *A New View of the Plays of Racine.* London: MacMillan, 1948. Unfortunately not new, then or now. The scene by scene analyses will bore all but the rankest beginners; it is only to these that this book is suggested.

POCOCK, GORDON. *Corneille and Racine. Problems of Tragic Form.* Cambridge: Cambridge Univ. Press, 1973. Debatable definitions lead to some very interesting insights into dramatic structure.

TOBIN, RONALD W. *Racine and Seneca.* Chapel Hill: Univ. of North Carolina Press, 1971. Goes well beyond the title. Subtle, yet easy to read.

TURNELL, MARTIN. *Jean Racine Dramatist.* London: Hamish Hamilton, 1972. Anything but subtle in form and content, and disregards everything that modern critics have contributed to the understanding of Racine, yet contagious enthusiasm may get some points across where the academic writings he derides might fail.

VINAVER, EUGENE. *Racine and Poetic Tragedy.* Manchester: Manchester Univ. Press, 1955. Technical yet easy to follow. Best attempt in

English to come to grasp with a subject, but a thorough knowledge of French will be needed to read it.

VOSSLER, KARL. *Jean Racine.* New York: Ungar, 1971. Translation of a book that first came out in 1926 but which is still one of the best attempts at presenting Racine to non-French speaking readers.

WEINBERG, BERNARD. *The Art of Jean Racine.* Chicago: Univ. of Chicago Press, 1963. Careful look at Racine's theater, play by play, but a rigid method and predictable conclusions tend to repel.

Index

Abraham, Claude, 160n13, 161n3 161n5, 162n5, 165n12, 167n8, 168n5
Adam, Antoine, 95, 107
Aeschylus, 35, 148
Alembert, Jean Le Rond d', 170n8
Angélique, Mère, 16
Aristophanes, 59-60, 62, 162n6-7
Aristotle, 11, 27, 31, 33, 156, 171n10
Arnauld d'Andilly, Robert, 20

Baïf, Lazare de, 28
Balzac, J.-L. Guez de, 29
Barrault, Jean-Louis, 169n13
Baron, 106
Barthes, Roland, 39, 54
Batson, Alan, 163n4, 165n14
Beaumarchais, P.-A. Caron de, 60
Bell, Marie, 108
Bénichou, Paul, 174
Bernardin, N.-M., 167n10
Bernhardt, Sarah, 108
Boieldieu, François Adrien, 170n4
Boileau, Nicolas, 11-12, 20-21, 59, 61, 65
Bossuet, Jacques Bénigne, 103
Bouillon, duchess of, 159n6
Brereton, Geoffrey, 174-175
Brody, Jules, 36, 38, 41, 161n11-12, 164n6, 173
Butler, Philip, 9, 157

Cabeen, David, 173
Camus, Jean, 30, 76, 154
Caylus, Mme de, 170n4
Champmeslé, Marie Desmares, called, 21, 95
Chapelain, Jean, 15
Cioranescu, Alexandre, 173, 175
Clarac, Pierre, 61, 162n2
Clark, A. F. B., 175
Cohen, Jules-Emile-David, 170n4

Colbert, Jean-Baptiste, 15, 18, 77
Coras, Jacques de, 19
Corneille, Pierre, 11-12, 16-19, 27-29, 31-35, 42, 45-46, 49, 55, 59, 65-66, 77, 79, 83, 89, 101-104, 108, 111, 115, 139, 155-56, 160n13, 161n3, 162n5, 164n4, 165n6, 167n3, 167n8, 168n5
Corneille, Thomas, 12, 16, 22, 33
Cruickshank, John, 174
Cyrano de Bergerac, Savinien de, 60

Descartes, René, 27
Desmarets de Saint-Sorlin, Jean, 16
Dubois, J., 173
Dubu, Jean, 59, 148, 162n3
Du Parc, Thérèse de Gorla, called, 17, 22
Edelman, Nathan, 169n15, 173
Edwards, Michael, 165n8, 166n9, 167n2, 170n6
Euripides, 29, 35, 122, 125, 168n10

Fergusson, Francis, 27, 160n12, 163n5, 171n2
Flaubert, Gustave, 154
France, Peter, 175
Freeman, Bryant, 163n4, 165n14
Furetière, Antoine, 59

Garapon, Robert, 62
Garnier, Robert, 28, 35
Geoffroy, Jean-Marie Michel, 103
Goethe, Johann Wolfgang von, 33, 133
Goldman, Lucien, 160n10
Gomberville, Marin Le Roy de, 45
Gossec, F.-J. Gossé, called, 170n4
Gravit, Francis W., 173
Grente, Georges, Cardinal, 173
Gross, Nathan, 64, 162n6
Guicharnaud, Jacques, 171n4
Gutwirth, Marcel, 54, 168n6, 169n11

177

Hardy, Alexandre, 28
Haydn, Franz Joseph, 170n4
Hazard, Paul, 26
Henrietta of England, 17, 18, 77
Hobbes, Thomas, 91
Homer, 103, 118, 120
Howard, W. D., 174
Hubert, Judd D., 39, 48, 57, 70, 91, 142, 168n13, 169n9, 170n2

James II of England, 24
James III of England, 24
Jasinski, René, 9
Jodelle, Etienne, 28

Kemp, Robert, 168n1
Klapp, Otto, 173
Knight, R. C., 30, 175
Koch, Philip, 126

La Fontaine, Jean de, 15
Lagane, R., 173
Lancaster, Henry C., 174
Lancelot, Claude, 13
Lapp, John, 37, 81, 164n8, 165n11, 167n11, 168n9, 168n12, 168n1, 170n5, 175
La Rochefoucauld, François de, 103, 108
Le Clerc, Michel, 19
Le Maître de Sacy, Isaac Lemaistre, called, 13, 20
Lough, John C., 160n4, 174
Louis XIV, 11, 15, 17, 19-24, 61, 77, 101, 135, 138, 144, 159n5, 170n4

Louvois, F.-M. Le Tellier de, 23, 138
Lully, Jean-Baptiste, 22
de Luynes (family), 14

Machiavelli, Niccolo, 91
Maintenon, Françoise d'Aubigné de, 23-24, 135, 138
Mairet, Jean, 32, 89
Mancini, Marie, 77
Maulnier, Thierry, 37, 125, 134, 168n2, 170n7
Mauron, Charles, 9
May, Georges, 27

Mazarin, Jules, Cardinal, 77, 159n6
Menander, 59
Molière, Jean-Baptiste Poquelin, called, 11, 15-20, 35, 59-60, 63-64, 130, 137, 155, 159n1, 162n8
Montchrestien, Antoine de, 28
Montespan, Françoise de, 23, 138
Moore, Will G., 174
Moreau, Jean-Baptiste, 23-24, 135-36, 148, 170n8
Morel, Jacques, 28
Mould, William A., 55-56
Mourgues, Odette de, 9, 160n14, 166n4, 175
Muir, Kenneth, 174-75

Nevers, duke of, 20, 159n6
Nicole, Pierre, 13
Nietzsche, Friedrich, 30
Nivers, 136

Orgel, Vera, 38, 175

Pascal, Blaise, 30, 103, 150
Pfohl, Russell, 168n4, 168n8, 168n14-15
Picard, Raymond, 9, 18, 21-24, 77, 90, 154, 165n5, 168n3, 174
Pocock, Gordon, 175
Pommier, Jean, 21, 137
Poulet, Georges, 49
Pradon, Jacques, 19-21

Quinault, Philippe, 16, 41, 110

Rabelais, François, 163n8
Racine, Jean
Abrégé de l'histoire de Port-Royal, 12, 25
Alexandre, 11, 15-16, 35, 40, *41-45*, 46, 49, 77, 83, 161n13-15, 161n3
Amasie, 11, 14
Andromaque, 11, 17, 23, *46-57*, 64-65, 67, 74-75, 77, 113, 118, 155-56, 161n1-5, 162n6-11
Athalie, 12, 24, 41, 113, 143, *144-54*, 170n1-8, 171n9-12
Bajazet, 11, 18, 67, *89-100*, 102, 108, 110, 113, 124, 137, 157, 165n14, 165n1-2, 166n3-13, 167n2

Index

Bérénice, 11, 18, 32-33, 67, *77-88*, 93, 107, 110, 118-19, 124, 131, 161n5, 164n1-4, 165n5-14, 167n8, 170n8
Britannicus, 9, 11, 17, 32, 64, *65-76*, 77, 80, 84, 89, 92, 128, 156, 163n1-5, 164n6-11, 167n2
Cantiques spirituels, 12, 25
La Chute de Phaeton, 22
Esther, 12, 22-24, 113, *135-43*, 144-45, 152, 160n13, 169n1, 170n2-8, 170n5
Hymns from the Roman Breviary, 12
Idylle sur la paix, 12, 22
Iphigénie, 12, 19, *112-21* 122-23, 131, 153, 157, 168n1-15
Lettres à l'auteur des "Imaginaires", 11, 16-17
Mémoires pour les Religieuses de Port-Royal des Champs, 12
Mithridate, 12, 18, *101-11*, 112, 138, 165n14, 166n1, 167n2-11, 170n8
Phèdre, 12, 19-22, 30-31, 77, 108, 113, 121, *122-34*, 141, 143, 154, 156, 162n4, 167n2, 168n1-2, 169n3-16, 170n8
Les Plaideurs, 11, 17, *58-64*, 76, 162n1-8, 163n9-15
La Thébaïde, 11, 15, *35-41*, 44, 70, 108, 119, 130, 160n1-3, 161n4-12
Théagène et Chariclée, 11, 14

Racine, Louis, 12, 22
Rawlings, Margaret, 160n9, 175
Regnard, Jean-François, 60
Rohou, Jean, 163n2
Romanet, Catherine de, 12
Rotrou, Jean de, 35-36

Saint-Aignan, duke of, 15

Saint-Evremond, Charles de, 16
Scherer, Jacques, 171n3
Seneca, 33, 35, 122, 159n1
Sévigné, Marie de Rabutin-Cantal de, 101, 135
Shakespeare, William, 26-27, 29-31, 41, 76, 160n9
Simonnet, André, 104
Soares, Sandra, 161n5, 165n12
Sophocles, 108, 156
Solomon, Samuel, 174
Starobinski, Jean, 30, 133, 163n6, 169n14
Statius, 35
Suetonius, 78
Sweetser, Marie-Odile, 76

Tacitus, 65
Taine, Hippolyte, 27
Terence, 65
Tobin, Ronald, 166n10, 169n3, 175
Tristan l'Hermite, François l'Hermite, called, 30, 32, 89
Turnell, Martin, 79, 161n13, 175

d'Urfé, Honoré, 45

Valincour, Jean Henry de, 159n9
Vier, Jacques, 117
Vinaver, Eugene, 175
Virgil, 46
Voltaire, François Marie Arouet, called, 137, 171n8
Vossler, Karl, 176

Webster, John, 26-27
Weinberg, Bernard, 176
William of Orange, 24

Yarrow, P. J., 39, 174